Praise for Good Enough Parent

There's a scene most Christian parents live inside without ever naming it: the slammed door, the silence in the car afterward, the private question that follows — *did I just fail as a parent, or worse, as a Christian? Good Enough Parent* doesn't flinch from that moment. It walks straight into it and says something most parenting books are too afraid to say: you don't have to win that moment to be a good parent. That's not a small claim. It's the kind of sentence that gets underlined, photographed, and sent to a friend at midnight.

— Hannah M.

The emphasis on the "Simple Uncluttered Gospel" was particularly powerful. The way the book centers unconditional love and removes the burden of shame sets this book apart from many other parenting resources. Each of the 18 tips felt thoughtful, actionable, and adaptable to real-life situations.

— Wice O.

Good Enough Parent is not another Christian parenting manual built on guilt, pressure, or the fantasy that the right formula will produce the right child. Its strength is that it begins where many parents actually live: tired, humbled, worried, and quietly wondering whether they have already failed.

— Chris M.

The book speaks to real parents dealing with real life. The focus isn't on being a perfect parent but on being a present, growing, and faith filled one. The advice is practical, encouraging, and easy to apply without making parents feel guilty for their mistakes. The overall message is one that many parents need to hear. Grace, consistency, and love matter more than getting everything right.

— Lillian

I found *Good Enough Parent* to be an absolute lifeline. Dr. Bill Senyard's refreshing blend of neuroscience, attachment theory, and the gospel completely shifted my perspective, but it was his shame-free reminder that we only need to get about 30% right that truly hit home for me. If you are a Christian parent navigating the messy, unpredictable waters of raising tweens or teens and feeling like you're constantly falling short, you will find immense hope, comfort, and practical wisdom in these pages.

— Esther

What stood out most to me was how *Good Enough Parent* seamlessly brought together the gospel, neuroscience, and personal storytelling. This combination not only made the book insightful but also incredibly relatable and practical.

— Bonny

What makes *Good Enough Parent* structurally different is that it refuses to hand readers a technique to master. Instead, it hands them a number — 30% — and lets that number do the theological work that most parenting books try to do with willpower and effort. You root grace in attachment science instead of leaving it as an abstract comfort, and that combination is rare. Most Christian parenting books either lean fully into neuroscience or fully into Scripture; you let them argue for the same conclusion at the same time, which gives skeptical readers a second door into the same truth.

— Hannah M.

I was immediately drawn to its refreshingly honest perspective. In a culture where parents are often surrounded by expectations and advice on how to do everything perfectly, the idea of embracing a more realistic and grace-filled approach feels both reassuring and deeply relevant.

— Sofya E.

In his book *Good Enough Parent*, Dr. Bill Senyard writes for Christian mothers and fathers raising teens whose reactions can change the mood of a home within minutes. His message begins with Jesus: God's love for a parent is secured before any parenting success appears. 5-Stars.

— Asher S. For Readers' Favorite

Good Enough Parent, to me, should be on the shelves of all Christian readers, particularly parents of adolescents. 5-Stars.

— Pekasho D. For Readers' Favorite

Good Enough Parent by Dr Bill Senyard is the kind of parenting book you didn't know you needed until the weight of raising a teenager finally humbles you. Written by a pastor and a once-teen parent, this book is structured in a common style called list form with a little twist. He combines three unconventional elements, such as the gospel, neuroscience, and storytelling, to deliver a core message on teen and tween parenting: the goal of Christian parenting is never perfection. 5-Stars.

— Karen T. for Readers Favorite

You have written something that weary Christian parents desperately need right now. Not want. Not might be interested in. Desperately need it.

— Elowen P.

I came across *Good Enough Parent* and found myself utterly captivated by the sheer honesty and transformative depth of this remarkable book. This is not simply another parenting guide; it is an extraordinary invitation to breathe, to let go of impossible pressure, and to discover that the goal of parenting was never perfection but a deeper dependence on Jesus. It is a book that dares to tell weary Christian parents the truth they desperately need to hear, and does so with a refreshing blend of biblical wisdom, neuroscience, and real-life experience that is rare in modern Christian publishing.

— Samuel J.

Books like this can provide not only practical guidance but also reassurance and encouragement to parents who may feel overwhelmed by the responsibilities they carry.

— Raj

Good Enough Parent explores the gap between exhausting perfectionism in parenting and the shame-free reality of being "good enough" through a gospel-centered lens. A natural fit for readers who connected with books such as *The Whole Brain Child*, *Parenting With Love and Logic*, and *Give Them Grace*, particularly because of its focus on attachment theory, neuroscience, and gospel-centered shame-free parenting for the overwhelmed parent of teens and tweens.

— Festus A.

Most parenting books pile on more pressure, more techniques, more guilt. You did the opposite.

— Enoch H.

On the surface, *Good Enough Parent* is a practical guide for raising teens and tweens. But the deeper I looked, the more it felt like a book about grace, both for children and for the parents raising them.

— Rachel S.

I was genuinely impressed by *Good Enough Parent's* compassionate and refreshing perspective on parenting. In a culture that often places impossible expectations on mothers and fathers, your emphasis on becoming a "good enough" parent rather than striving for perfection offers a message that feels both liberating and deeply needed.

— Shelby V.

Good Enough Parent directly counters the performance-driven perfectionism that leaves so many Christian families feeling burnt out.

— Avery M.

Praise for On-Line Good Enough Parent (www.goodenoughparent.online)

"My child isn't isolating as much. I am more relaxed as a parent and asking God to direct my words with my child." -- Tracy H.

"I really appreciated the non-shaming approach Dr. Senyard took to this information." — Amy V

"Personally, your research and your work really resonates with me. The dynamics of attachment theory and the connections of the Inner Working Models helps me to have greater understanding as I continue to build my relationship with my 21-year-old daughter."— Ann J

"Pausing and taking time to listen apply these things in my life and learn to depend on the Holy Spirit for parenting!!" — Bridget P

"I found the tips regarding brain development and attachment styles to be very helpful. Reasoning with a brain that's still developing usually doesn't go well!" —Amy V

"This whole program was exactly what I needed. The most beneficial reminder was that I just need to get 30% right to be a good enough parent."—Tracy H

"Understanding why they might do the things they do; it's not all their fault; realizing the importance of constantly telling our children how much we love them and are proud of them." —E. C.

"This phrase—good enough— highlighted the perfectionism I didn't realize I was full of. Also, it replaced it with a more gracious measure of seeing where there was progress. Just hearing you say the phrase "good enough" every day for two weeks helped plant it in my brain and heart." —Susan A

Good Enough Parent

Simple Biblical Tips For Imperfect Parents Raising Real Kids

Dr. Bill Senyard

This book is dedicated to all who helped me survive parenting.
To my beloved wife, Eunice. She not only shared this joyful journey
with me but has served as the editor of this project.
To my three wonderful children—now adults—who, by the grace of
God, seem mostly okay. Though I remain fairly certain each of them
has needed counseling at some point... and if not, probably should.
But most of all, to God—Father, Son, and Spirit—whose love for the
unlovable, the unloved, the unlovely, the unlikely, and the unworthy
rescued me long ago... and kept rescuing me on the many days my
parenting failed to reflect His heart.
All praise to God Almighty—
the only truly Good Enough Parent.

Contents

Introduction

Welcome, battle-weary Christian parent.

Did you know that your child's brain is constantly trying to answer two questions? Wouldn't it be helpful to know what those questions are? You will find out in the *Good Enough Parent* book.

Parenting teens and tweens can be brutal—extremely brutal.

Puberty hits, peer pressure seeps in from everywhere, social media has a very dark side, and then throw in pandemics, cultural chaos and polarization, economic swings, and the eternal mystery of why every roll of toilet paper disappears the week your kid has friends over.

One writer described adolescence like this: "It felt like my child had walked past a leaking nuclear reactor."

All parents feel what you are feeling.

We are out of our wheelhouse, trying to keep up. Still, it often seems we go from conflict to conflict, from blowup to blowup, from disobedience to disobedience—and there is little we can do to stop it.

It feels like driving without a steering wheel—or without

brakes. The way we were raised seems irrelevant. Things have dramatically changed, and we can't get off the steep learning curve.

Most of us are just trying to survive—relationally, emotionally, financially—while wondering if we're permanently scarring our children.

And then there's Proverbs 22:6 hanging over our heads almost like a continuous cosmic performance review: "Train up a child in the way he should go; even when he is old he will not depart from it."

Solomon, have you met my child?

You will hear me speak of the *Good Enough Parent*. But what counts as success—80%? 75%? Did I already blow it back in middle school?

Attachment psychologists talk about the *good enough parent*—the parent who gets it right about 30% of the time.[1] Thirty percent! That feels doable on a Tuesday.

What does *getting it right* mean for Christian parents? And what does a good enough Christian parent look like? Those are the topics I will cover in *Good Enough Parent*.

Here's the truth we all need to hear on repeat:

Only God is the Perfect Parent. You and I will never be perfect parents. That's not an achievable goal.

This book offers 18 concise, shame-free tips grounded in biblical principles, neuroscience, attachment theory, and the gospel —all designed to help you become a more *Good Enough Parent (GEP)*.

Applying just a few of these manageable tips can bring mean-

---

1. Ratnapalan, Savithiri, and Helen Batty. 2009. "To Be Good Enough." *Canadian Family Physician / Médecin de famille canadien* 55, no. 3: 239–42.

ingful, encouraging progress (not perfection) in your parenting journey.

Here are reviews of the online *Good Enough Parent*:

"I loved the repeated message, we are not trying to be more like God, we are trying to depend upon Him more."

"I am now more able to take a step back when we have arguments and not get so offended by what my daughter is saying."

"This whole program was exactly what I needed. The most beneficial reminder was that I just need to get 30% right to be a good enough parent."

Frustrated Christian parent, you're not alone. Take a deep breath —in through the nose and exhale slowly through your mouth as your shoulders relax.

You're in a safe place here.

The *Good Enough Parent* book covers the same tips as the online version (www.goodenoughparent.online).

Good news! I have added three additional special tips for our book audience.

How to use this book

For 30 days, try three or four tips that resonate with you and that fit within your context. The results might surprise and encourage you on your parenting journey.

Scan the QR code or go to the website to hear a testimony from a couple who has gone through the online version of GEP. Enjoy.

Welcome, parent, guardian, caregiver, to *Good Enough Parent.*

Tip #1
Good Enough Parents Experience the Simple, Uncluttered Gospel More Than Non-Good-Enough Parents

Welcome to Tip #1 in this fifteen-tip journey toward becoming a Good Enough Parent (GEP)—or at least to becoming a *more* good enough parent (apologies for the grammar).

Good news, parents! You can begin to incorporate this tip immediately. No special skills or five-page IKEA instructions are required.

We all suffer from a universal human problem. Many of us don't think we are good enough—or we are afraid that we are messing up our teens—or that Jesus is looking down and shaking his head when he sees what we are doing. Consequently, we feel ashamed, like a disappointment, afraid, and maybe even depressed.

Context is important: You have two people—you and your child—with two beat-up brains, checkered histories, two emotionally strained neural wirings, two often defensive, reactionary triggers, and two walking experimental laboratories—sometimes dealing with very toxic chemicals. It is a recipe for mess-ups—every day—24/7.

Hear this, tattoo it to your arm if you must. "It is not all your or your child's fault."

You are not alone. We all need help, beyond reading the next book, Instagram reel, or that next expensive weekend conference that ends up making us feel worse.

Virtually all other Christian parenting programs think that our goal is to become more like Jesus. That's a good thing. But honestly, that goal can be very shaming. Who has cleared that ridiculously high bar? Or even come close? Am I right?

Jesus wasn't holding back in his Sermon on the Mount.

"Be perfect, therefore, as your heavenly Father is perfect." (Matt 5:48)

In context, "Be a perfect parent, as your heavenly Father is perfect."

How's it going?

Every parent has failed to clear that bar. GEP believes that the correct response to Jesus' bold overarching command is a humble and accurate, "What? I can't do that."

Exactly. And no doubt, Jesus knew that. In fact, that is why he came. Not to teach us and shame us into perfection—that has never worked—but to help us see that we can't do it on our own.

The immediate goal for all of us is not to set our sights on being God-perfect. That strategy is a well-meaning rabbit hole that was pursued by the people who assassinated Jesus rather than those who followed him. Don't misunderstand, in Heaven, we will be perfected. That too will be accomplished by God, not by us trying harder.

So, what are we to do? Just stop trying to be like Jesus? Yes and no. A better path to becoming better Jesus followers is to begin by bowing our heads, opening our empty hands, and confessing our need. We are imperfect vessels who need a rescuer.

Did you know that Jesus innately loves the unlovable, the unloved, the unlovely, the unworthy and the unlikely, and that's all of us on any given day if we were just a little bit honest—even parents.

GEPs understand that our God-ordained goal is, first and foremost, to become more *dependent* on Jesus. Growing in dependence on Him naturally results in us becoming more like Him. Doesn't that make sense? Remember, trying to become like Jesus versus becoming more dependent on Him and His Spirit are two very different strategies. Breathe. Relax your shoulders. Breathe again. Dependence on Jesus is the key to confident, relaxed parenting—not striving to be perfect.

Every one of our tips will emphasize the goal of "depending on Jesus and His Spirit more," not just trying harder. Anyone can depend; anyone can need.

Bottom line and good to say up front, *you have already messed it up.* God is perfect, and we're not—join the club.

But this should not lead to shame. Why? Good Enough Parents are beginning to experience the *Simple Uncluttered Gospel (SUG).* Here it is.

Jesus-Follower, Parent or Guardian, because of what Jesus did for you 2000 years ago, God loves you. He loves you fully—as much as the Father loves the Son and the Son loves the Father. He cannot love you more than He does right now. He will not love you less—whether you think you've been a good enough parent or not. He loves you as you are —not as you should be or could be. You cannot add to this love or take away from it. I get it—it often feels like you've messed it up, or that you need to do something so God will like you more. Not so. So how do you experience this love more now?

Simple. Ask. Take small, daily steps. Ask the Spirit inside you to make you know, experience, and feel how much God loves you—right now. Ask again later today. Ask tomorrow. Make it a habit.

These concepts are further unpacked and applied in the free online experiential path, *The Dance (www.the-dance.org).*

Jesus-followers are all a part of that dance—but for many of us, we haven't felt it in a long time. Some Christians can't even hear the music anymore.

The online *Dance* is designed for all those Christians—including weary parents who feel like disappointments to Jesus—falling short of standards, lacking faith, and hearing a screaming inner critical voice that says "you don't measure up to others."

Where does the concept of the dance come from? Gregory of Nazianzus, the Archbishop of Constantinople in the late 4th century, while attempting to describe the inner nature of God, used the Greek verb, *perichoreo*. Literally, it is *peri*-around and *choreo*-dance.

He imagined the Father, Son, and Spirit in a very personal, joyous, engaging dance-around. The Greek carries the subtle nuance of not just an exclusive dance, but one that uniquely makes room for other faulty, rescued people like you and me.

Even struggling parents.

Even their teens and tweens.

Jonathan Marlowe helpfully wrote in *The Dance of the Trinity*:

If any of you have ever been to a Greek wedding, you may have seen their distinctive way of dancing… It's called *peri-choresis*. There are not two dancers, but at least three. They start to go in circles, weaving in and out in this very beautiful pattern of motion. They start to go faster and faster and faster, all the while staying in perfect rhythm and in sync with each other. Eventually, they are dancing so quickly (yet so effortlessly) that as you look at them, it just becomes a blur. Their individual identities are part of a larger dance. The early church fathers and mothers looked at that dance (*perichoresis*) and said, 'That's what the Trinity is like.'... This relationship is called love, and it's what the Trinity is all about. The *perichoresis* is the dance of love.[1]

This dance is happening now. Fellow believer, you already have the Spirit in you, so you are a part of that dance. You can't be partly in it or on probation. But you are not alone if you're feeling disconnected from it.

Parents can be very distracted and feel beaten up. I want to help you experience the dance more today—and tomorrow. It will make a huge difference in your parenting journey—your identity, your other relationships, your sense of well-being, your joy.

Parents, no matter how good or not good enough you've been recently, specifically because of what Jesus did for you 2000 years ago, God adores you.

This bears repeating. You can't add to God's adoration of you by being a better parent or mess it up by falling short of perfection today.

No shaming intended, you are not a perfect parent.

You have messed it up.

You have fallen short—and yet,

you are still not a disappointment to Jesus.

There is also no need for shame in your relationship with God, with Jesus, with the Spirit—ever. Their love for you can never be diluted. God's face still lights up when He sees you (humanly speaking).

---

1. Marlowe, Jonathan. "The Dance of the Trinity (Perichoresis: The Dance of Love)." Grace Communion International, sermon transcript / teaching article, n.d.

I get it, that critical voice in your head—I call mine "the beast" —will tell you that it is not safe to look up into the face of God. That is a lie.

Say the Simple Uncluttered Gospel aloud at least twice a day.

Think of it this way. When you say it aloud, you are witnessing to that nasty, critical voice in your head that has been running amok and oozing poison-laced criticism into your brain. "How can Jesus be happy with you after all of the mistakes and bad choices you've made?"

The question is powerfully misleading. You have the favor of Christ because he purchased it for you, for all time. His love is innate for failures. That's all there is. By saying the *Simple Uncluttered Gospel (SUG)* aloud to your midbrain, you become a missionary to that unreached people group living in your head and its town crier, that critical inner voice.

Unfortunately, you will have that critical voice until you die. You will die with it, not from it. We can't get rid of it, but we can displace it with a different, louder voice.

According to neuroscience, the way to get its attention is through a repetitive drip, drip, drip and a daily verbal proclamation of the gospel (*SUG*).

How many times should you do this? For me, I need it two or three times daily—just saying.

I recommend saying it aloud twice a day until your child notices something has changed. Begin today.

No parent survives without feeling like a failure at times, maybe often. And it goes downhill from there. Subconsciously, we become blaming, self-critical, defensive, enraged, or even depressed. That does not help our cause.

If you were to look up and see the face of God right now, you *would* see great joy—you *would* see His eyes dilate because he is so jazzed by looking into your face. He can't wait to spend eternity with you—face to face. Think of the good Father running to embrace the wayward, "prodigal" son or daughter.

I will say more, but if you can see that your struggle is with your mid-brain and that critical inner voice, doesn't that help explain your child? Children have the same issue. So much of what they say and do, or do not say and do not do, is not all their fault.

For instance, during adolescence, your child's brain is an emotional, spiritual blender. Teens and tweens are often not being rational or reasonable.

You can't fix them. You've been trying, and no doubt it hasn't worked well. You can't access their midbrain or pull on some lever or something like a TV remote to reduce cortisol and other powerful chemicals that are causing chaos.

What is your brain learning as you immerse yourself in the *Simple Uncluttered Gospel*? God loves sinners. He loves failures. He loves imperfect people. He even loves non-good-enough parents. You may not have heard it this way before but think about it.

That's all there is.

In fact, He dances with them.

And this intimate and powerful experience of the height, width, length, and depth of the love of Christ for you, right now, as you are, will begin to make you a better, good enough parent—at least a little bit.

A little less reactionary,

a little less lonely,

a little less a failure,

less depressed,

less ashamed,

—a parent who doesn't need your child's love and appreciation as much.

It is an important start. In fact, it is foundational.

So, what can you do? Simple. Do you want to be a more *good enough parent*? Ask the Spirit to make you feel God's adoration of you a little more today than yesterday. It will be noticeable. It will make a difference.

For your convenience, *Good Enough Parent Simple Uncluttered Gospel Bookmarks* are available from the website (www.gospel-app.com). Place them all over the house as a constant reminder.

Tip #2

Good Enough Parents Access the Power of the Gospel More Than Non-Good-Enough Parents

(You don't innately have this power.
God is overjoyed to give you His love for the unlovable,
unloved, unlovely, unworthy, and unlikely
—just ask.)

If parenting teens were simply reasonable adults negotiating life with smaller, slightly less reasonable humans, we might stand a chance. But very little about adolescence is reasonable.

You probably already knew that.

Check out the imagine on the next page.

I use this "Gospel App Shape" for the two spiritual-formation, discipleship curricula: *Gospel App* and, for young adults, *Take Heart YZ*. (Available on Amazon.)

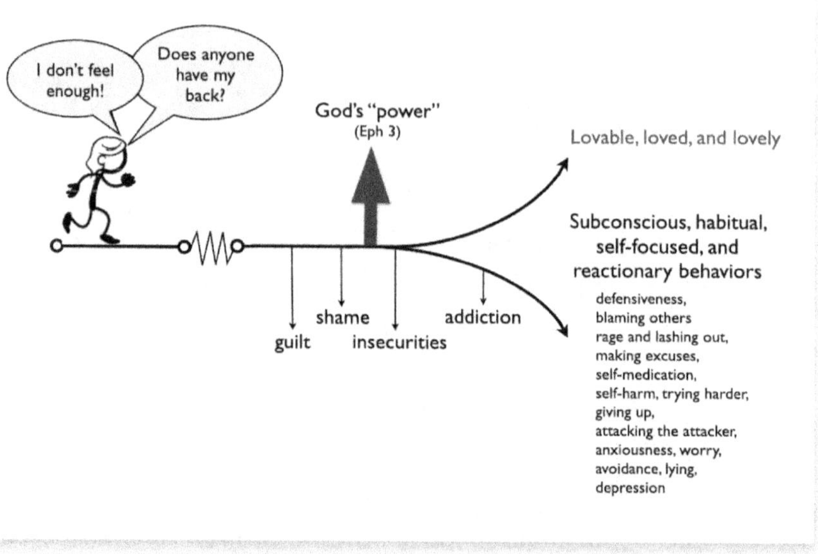

Your son or daughter is "Stick," the groaning figure on the far left. They are wondering if they are enough (I will say more about that in a future tip). Are they good enough, attractive enough, funny enough, woke enough, smart enough in your eyes, the eyes of others, and the mirror? We all wonder, but never more than when we are adolescents. The implied answer for so many teens is, "Nope, probably not." You may be wondering the very same thing as you look in the mirror. I get it.

Follow the path (the arrow) down and to the right. That is the landing place of normal, human, self-focused, reactionary behaviors: anxiety, depression, rage, identity issues, loneliness, and isolation. You get the idea. You've probably seen some of these things in your child—and in *your* mirror.

It gets worse. Notice the four downward arrows tugging at Stick. These are the same four powers that act on your child's brain 24/7—mainly subconsciously.

There is *guilt*:

"I've messed up. I did something wrong that I am not proud of. I feel bad about it."

There is *shame*. Worse than guilt.

"Not only did I do something wrong, clearly, I am wrong. I am a disappointment to my family and to God. I will never measure up. I lack *enoughness* and the hope for connectedness."

There's more. There are *insecurities*. Think of an orphaned child on a city street. They believe that no one has their back. They are on their own. At the end of the day, they believe that their sense of significance, security, and belonging depends entirely on their efforts that day. They don't trust institutions or others, for the most part, so they are isolated and alone. They use authority, but don't trust authority.

Lastly, there are *addictions*. Don't just think opioids, alcohol, or crack. The addictions could be social media, gaming, athletics, cutting, and so many more. In our shape, such self-medication serves to mask the emotional pain that comes from guilt, shame, and insecurities. This is the thing or person we run to in order to get rid of the pain of our sense of not-enoughness and disconnectedness (our euphemisms for shame and loneliness).

These four subconscious forces—not under the control of the rational part of the brain—exacerbate the downward tailspin of your child today, tomorrow, and the next day. This is true for every child. It's equally true for adults.

But what can Good Enough Parents do?

Romans 8 is one of the richest chapters in the entire Bible, and the "groaning" section (verses 18–27) is the emotional and theological high point for every Christian parent of teens who feels like the wheels are coming off the bus.

Paul wrote that all creation groans (Rom 8:22). That is *all*— every. That includes your tween and teen's brain, your brain, your family's, your conversations, your relationships, your in-laws, their peers, and your peers—lots of groaning is happening.

Paul uses the Greek word *stenazō* (to groan, sigh deeply) three separate times in nine verses—like a triple bell ringing over a broken world, a broken body, and a broken family.

Here are the three *groans* and why they hit parents right in the chest.

1. Creation Groans (v. 22)

"We know that the whole creation has been groaning together in the pains of childbirth until now." Rom 8:22

- The entire created order is pictured as a woman in labor —intense pain, but pain with a purpose.
- Every hurricane, every school shooting, every social media algorithm designed to hook your kid's brain, every hormonal meltdown at 10 p.m.—it's all part of the birth pangs.
- Your teenager's chaos is not random; it's inside the biggest story ever told. Their world is not dying; it is being born.

For parents, this is massive: the eye-rolling, the slammed doors, the "I hate you," the secret cutting, the lying, the porn, the identity confusion—none of it is a sign that the universe is collapsing. It is evidence of a new creation fighting to get out. Your job is to manifest Jesus' Spirit into the mix as much as possible.

2. We Ourselves Groan (v. 23)

"And not only the creation, but we ourselves, who have the first fruits of the Spirit, groan inwardly as we wait eagerly for adoption as sons, the redemption of our bodies." Rom 8:23

- Even Spirit-filled Christians groan.
- Paul is not talking about unbelievers here—he's talking about people who have tasted the first fruits (the Holy Spirit living inside).
- If you love Jesus and still want to lock your teenager in the basement sometimes until they're 30, congratulations —first, don't do it; second, you're normal. Paul says that groaning is built in until the resurrection.

Paul bookends the first two groanings with rocket fuel for discouraged parents:

"For I consider that the sufferings of this present time are not worth comparing with the glory that is to be revealed to us." Rom 8:18

The teenage decade feels like forever, but in light of eternity, it is a blink. The slammed doors, the identity crises, the scary Google search history—none of it gets the final word.

And then:

"For in this hope we were saved… But if we hope for what we do not see, we wait for it with patience." Rom 8:24–25

Your child's story is not finished. Your family's story is not finished. The resurrection is coming—new bodies, new hearts, a new heaven and a new earth. Until then, we groan, we wait, we hope—and the Spirit groans with us.

Parenting translation:

That ache in your chest when you see your kid hurting, that exhaustion when another boundary is ignored, that grief when they walk away from the faith you tried to give them—that is the groan of someone who may have the Spirit but has yet to become what they will be.

3. The Spirit Groans (vv. 26–27)

The third groaning is also good news for parents.

"Likewise the Spirit helps us in our weakness. For we do not know what to pray for as we ought, but the Spirit himself intercedes for us with groanings too deep for words. And he who searches hearts knows what is the mind of the Spirit, because the Spirit intercedes for the saints according to the will of God." Rom 8:26-27

- The most mind-blowing part: when you are so tired or confused that you have zero words left (11:07 p.m., lights off, staring at the ceiling after the fight), the Holy Spirit inside you is praying on your behalf with groans deeper than human language.
- Those sighs, those wordless tears, that "Jesus… please…" that you can barely whisper—the Spirit takes them, translates them perfectly, and carries them straight to the Father's throne.
- Your children are in good hands—just not yours.

Parenting translation

When you've run out of wisdom, when every parenting book has failed, when you literally don't know what to pray for your child anymore—you are not alone in the room. The third person of the Trinity is groaning with you and for you, and those groans carry real weight.

One Sentence Takeaway for Parents of Teens

The next time your house feels like a war zone, and you're convinced you're failing, hear the triple groan of Romans 8: Creation says, "This hurts, but it's birth, not death." Your own heart says, "I'm not home yet." And the Holy Spirit says, "I've got you—and I've got your kid—and My groans are perfect prayers."

That is why good enough parents go to bed, exhale, and can finally sleep—because the worst nights are still inside the best story, and the Spirit never stops groaning until the story is complete.

Your son or daughter is caught in a brutal downward spiral driven by four forces that pull harder than gravity: guilt, shame, insecurities, and addictions. Those four forces don't take days off.

But where can parents turn for a power that's stronger?

Let me take you to Ephesus, around AD 60–62.

Ephesus was the Vegas of the first-century Roman Empire—glittering temples, non-stop commerce, the massive temple of Artemis (one of the Seven Wonders), rampant sexual immorality, and a mob of artisans getting rich off little silver Artemis shrines. Christians were a tiny, often despised minority. They were mocked, excluded, sometimes beaten, and occasionally killed.

Their kids were growing up in a culture that hated everything they believed in.

Sound familiar?

Paul is sitting in a Roman prison (probably under house arrest) when he writes to those stressed-out believers. He knows their lives are difficult. He knows parenting in that environment feels impossible. And in the middle of his letter, he drops to his knees and prays one main thing—the same thing we need today.

Ephesians 3:14–21 (my paraphrase with emphasis):

For this reason I kneel before the Father… I pray that out of His glorious riches He may strengthen you with **power** through His Spirit in your inner being, so that Christ may dwell in your hearts through faith. And I pray that you, being rooted and established in love, may have **power**… to grasp how wide and long and high and deep is the love of Christ… and to know this love that surpasses knowledge—that you may be filled to the measure of all the **fullness of God**. Now to him who is able to do immeasurably more than all we ask or imagine, according to his **power** that is at work within us, to him be glory in the church and in Christ Jesus throughout all generations, for ever and ever! Amen. (Eph 3:14-21)

Note what he asks for. Three times, Paul will mention *power* in this short section—two different Greek words. This power doesn't come from the Ephesians. He is *not* suggesting that they need to work harder. It turns out that they don't have that muscle group. Only God has it. It is not on their shoulders. No shame.

Parents, you desperately need God's heaven-sourced power to pull off good enough parenting. I repeat, this is not trying harder; this is depending more upon God.

How?

Paul asks on their behalf that they receive God's power (which should be noticeable) through the means of the Spirit in their inner being (wherever that is).

Think of a pipeline from your inner being (somewhere in your brain) to the power storehouse of God.

Remember, in the last tip, I said that our goal is not to make you more *like* Jesus, but rather to make you more *dependent* upon Him and His Spirit. Here it is in Biblical print. How have we missed it?

Paul is modeling the secret sauce right in front of us: *we ask, God gives*. A child can do it. A prison-chain-wearing apostle does it.

A frustrated, bleary-eyed parent at 11:03 p.m. after the third fight of the night can do it. I can do it.

What exactly am I asking for?

1. Power that makes me aware of Christ's favor in my heart (instead of constantly wondering if He's moved out because of today's failures).
2. Power to grasp—really grasp, emotionally—the endless dimensions of Christ's love for me—exactly as I am… and for my prickly, dysregulated teen exactly as they are. This is important. I am asking for God's love for my teen through me.
3. Power to have my identity reservoir filled with the fullness of God so that I feel "good enough."

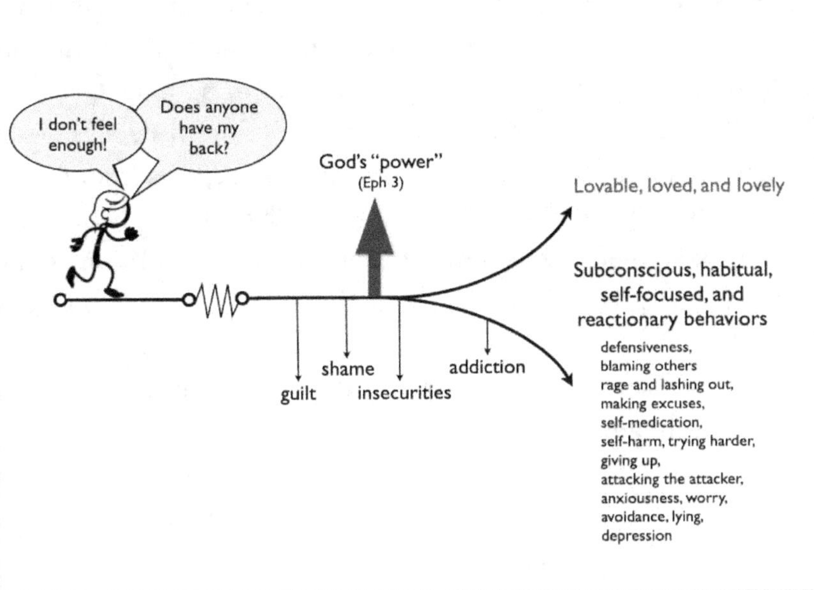

GEPs, to love others—like your child—who spends so much time in the lower right-hand of the "Gospel App Shape," who have hormones and chemicals ripping through their brain, and who are often emotionally dysregulated, you will need to have your identity cup filled—a little. You can't depend on your child to fill your cup. That is perhaps the #1 mistake parents make.

Have you ever walked away from an argument with your spouse or child and felt empty? Powerless? You're not alone. I think the fullness of God gives parents a deeper reservoir to love the unlovable. Ultimately, this is just you tapping into God's deepness. You have some new and better resiliency.

Don't think Valentine's type love, think about the love of God that by nature loves failures, the beat up, and those who feel they are not enough, those who are in a reactionary, destructive tailspin right now.

To be clear, you and I have a real problem. We have essentially been unaware that we desperately need an ongoing power from God to even begin to feel His love for ourselves and our teens because our brains are so relationally beat-up, scarred and maybe even cynical. Nothing has hurt us more than relationships, nothing. Our brain has built subconscious fortresses to protect us from being hurt by love again—but the nasty side effect is that it keeps us from feeling loved and from feeling unguarded love for others.

I chuckle when I see so many people reading books on setting boundaries. It's like Tiger Woods reading a book on *The Basics of Golf.* Your brain is a master at setting boundaries. Boundaries are designed to keep you from being hurt—but they also can prevent you from feeling loved.

Here's the point. Jesus loves you 100%, but your brain is so messed up, it can't or won't let you feel it totally. You don't have the capacity to turn off the boundaries or to make your brain feel loved. If we had that, pharmaceutical stocks would plummet.

In his letter to the Ephesians, Paul makes it clear that you and I need to access God's power daily, specifically so you begin to feel the love of God for you as you are, and your teen as they are. That would be noticeable. Not perfectly—that's Heaven—but noticeably.

Have you ever heard that? You need to ask daily for God's power even to begin to feel the love of Jesus for you and others. It's true.

Parents, hear this loud and clear: Jesus secured 100% of God's love for you on the cross. But our brains are so scarred by decades of relational hurt that we need supernatural power just to let that love land. We don't have that power. God does. And He loves to give it to parents who ask.

That's why the *Simple Uncluttered Gospel* (see Tip #1) always ends with a *MAKE ME* prayer. When you say it out loud (especially when you feel least lovable), you're doing exactly what Paul did for the Ephesians—and what the Spirit is still doing for us.

Keep saying it aloud twice a day, and you will likely notice a difference: Less reactivity. More resiliency. A growing ability to love when it makes no sense.

That's the power of the gospel—accessed the Ephesians way.

Good enough parents don't try harder; they ask continually with emptier hands.

Tip #3

Good Enough Parents Understand Their Own Brain More Than Non-Good-Enough Parents

(You're not nearly as reasonable as you think, and that's normal.)

So far, we have learned that good enough parents (GEPs) understand the *Simple Uncluttered Gospel (SUG)* better and preach it to their own midbrain often. They are accessing God's power to be loved and to love others a little more—at least in baby-steps. It takes time to build a habit. You can do this. You will notice a difference.

Imagine a scale of 0-10: GEPs understand what is happening in their own brain—maybe 10%—and I am being gracious here; it is probably closer to 1%. Scientists agree that our brains remain an unexplored continent in so many ways. We are learning more every day, but much of how our brains work remains a mystery.

The following illustration is a bit of an oversimplification. Yet it is helpful to see our brain as composed of two parts, two emphases —the emotional brain and the rational brain.

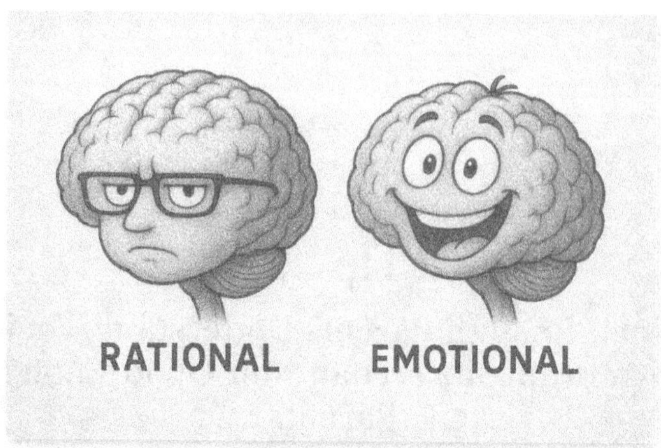

Are you familiar with the original Star Trek television series? Remember the contrast between Captain James T. Kirk, who was highly emotional, and the computer-like Spock, who was half Vulcan, half human and regularly struggled with residual human emotions? Emotional brain versus the rational brain.

Western civilization tends to worship our rational brain almost exclusively—it rules.

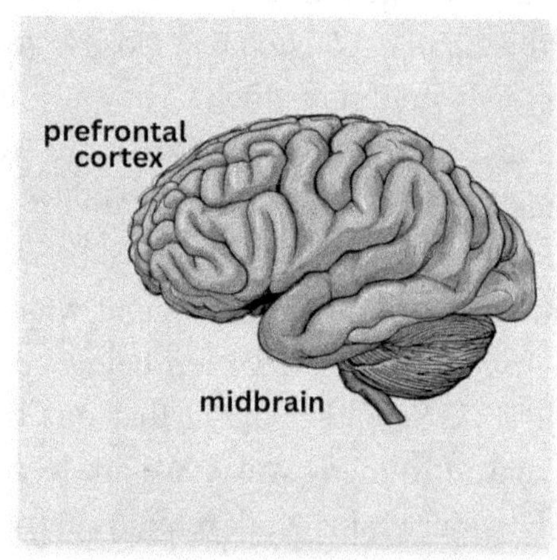

Queen of Reason: the prefrontal cortex.

The *prefrontal cortex*, just behind our forehead, is responsible for strategic thinking, abstract thought, moderating behavior, reasoning, decision-making, and considering the long-term consequences of choices. Some have described the *prefrontal cortex* as the carburetor for empathy, emotional desires, and risk-taking. Others have described it as the brain's emotional brakes. It asks, "Wait a minute, is that such a good idea?" It's important to have.

As Westerners, we have a shameful love affair with our prefrontal cortex. Historically, this comes from the Enlightenment —recall the adage, "I think, therefore I am." It turns out that this was a bit of an overstatement. Yet our entire education system is based upon the capabilities of our prefrontal cortex.

Think about it. We have counselors when our emotions are out of whack—but where do we go when our reason and logic are out of control? Washington? How many times in the last month have you cried out in frustration with your teen, "Just be reasonable!" Did you ever say, "Can you just be more emotional here?" Culturally, things are changing a bit, but still:

1. We revere reason over emotion.
2. We value reasonable people and are concerned about emotional ones.
3. We think that we are more reasonable than we probably are.
4. We are shocked when our teens aren't reasonable.

We think our brains are being reasonable—particularly when stress pummels us. We want to believe our prefrontal cortex is in complete control, like Spock, calling all the shots, and the emotion-packed midbrain is submitting to its authority. GEPs understand that it is not so clear based on the latest neuroscience.[1]

The prefrontal cortex is one of the weakest areas of our brain. Who knew? You've heard of chemicals and hormones that kick our brain into action at almost light speed, like dopamine, oxytocin, and cortisol—potent chemicals that are released when triggered by stress in the midbrain.

The prefrontal cortex has almost no chemicals. In fact, when your emotional mid-brain triggers and cortisol is released—you've heard of the fear cycle: fight, flight, or freeze—your prefrontal cortex is effectively shut down—offline.

When a mountain lion attacks you, you don't want to gather data, weigh options, consider long-term consequences and then act. No, you want immediate fight, flight or freeze. So, your body lights up Kirk and turns off Spock.

So, forget mountain lions, what happens when your teen talks back to you again? Or disobeys? Boom. Automatic fight, flight, or freeze. It is subconscious and happens at light speed.

So GEPs understand that when these difficult interactions happen with your teen, spouse, partner, boss, or anyone, you will be *less* reasonable and *more* reactive and emotional than you might imagine.

GEPs realize that even when you think you are being reasonable, the very opposite may be true. You believe you are channeling the calm, rational Spock, but your child is getting pummeled by James T. Kirk.

This does not make you a bad, weak, or broken person. It means you are human. Here's a test. Have you ever stood there while a surprising string of words comes out of your mouth—and even you are shocked to hear them? Before that moment, you would have

---

1. Siegel, Daniel J. *The Whole-Brain Child*. Delacorte Press, 2011; Schore, Allan N. "The Right Brain Is Dominant in Psychotherapy." *Psychotherapy*, vol. 51, no. 3, 2014, pp. 388–397.

sworn that you would never say that. But you just did. Something went around your prefrontal cortex. So much for reason-dominance.

To be clear, there are no muscle groups to manage your emotional mid-brain. Its workings are largely unconscious and automatic. Thus, trying harder won't work.

Your emotional mid-brain will trigger and react from powerful chemicals when you get that call from the principal to come and get your child, or your child sneaks porn, or yells disrespectfully at you in public, or storms out of the room when you are talking to them, or rolls their eyes, or gets arrested with drugs. In that moment, you are not going to be as reasonable as you would like to think—though you will swear that you are the pinnacle of Spockian calmness.

GEPs are a little more aware that they are not as reasonable and rational as they may feel. We call them blind spots for a reason.

Without the Spirit's indwelling, GEPs can *only* react. Spirit-indwelt GEPs may react as well, but they also have a competing power inside them.

It turns out that parents who are:

- accessing power from God through the Spirit in their inner being (Eph 3:14-21);
- regularly asking for God's power and are beginning to feel the height, width, length and depth of the love of Christ for them and their child;
- feeling the fullness of God in their emptied cup

have a new, legitimate choice. It should be noticeable. Does that make sense?

So, GEP, keep saying the *Simple Uncluttered Gospel* at least twice a day. Think of it as shaping a new positive habit. You will be glad you did.

I am following a logical progression. In the next tip, what in the world is happening inside my child's brain?

Good news and bad news.

Tip #4
Good Enough Parents Understand Their Teen's Brain More Than Non-Good-Enough Parents

(It's not totally their fault—adolescence is a decade-long, chemically-induced rebuild with the brakes missing. What could go wrong?)

If you want to be more of a GEP, doing the same things you've been doing more often isn't going to cut it.

The 18 tips in this book are here to help.

Find the ones that work for you and lean into them. In my experience, people who have committed to applying these tips have reported a positive change. I believe it might work for you, too.

Please hear this important public service announcement: Your teen is not a mini-adult.

Their prefrontal cortex (the brakes) won't finish construction until age 22–25. But the gas pedal—hormones, dopamine, sex drive, fear circuits—is wide open and fully operational.

Therefore, you don't need to take it personally when your child dysregulates, blows up, throws a fit, is unreasonable, disrespectful, disobedient, doesn't consider long-term consequences when making risky decisions, or seems to be addicted to anything that moves or doesn't move.

Non-GEPs might say something like, "If I did that to my parents...whew!"

Disrespected Non-GEPs tend to get angry, judgmental, bossy, resentful, condescending, contemptuous, and yes, even shaming.

In their brains, they will likely feel justified, inadequate, lost, like failures, weak, embarrassed, ashamed, and attacked. Understandable.

GEPs seem to understand a little more that it is not *all* their child's fault.

GEPs understand their teen's and tween's brains a little more than Non-GEPs.

Remember when we looked at the adult brain and described it as an ongoing conflict or balancing act between the rational and emotional parts?

Spock and James T. Kirk, the emotions and reactionary behaviors of the midbrain, in contrast to the calm, reasonable actions of the prefrontal cortex?

GEPs understand their teens' brains are very different.

Their prefrontal cortex is not fully online until the early 20s for girls and mid-20s for boys.

That's scary, right?

Think Blender

In adult brains, I spoke about triggers and cycles with the prefrontal cortex being the carburetor or the brakes of the car. It made some sense. But for tweens and teens, picture an emotional blender—new and exciting chemicals and hormones—with no brakes.

Look, I have a respectful beef with God. This design doesn't make any sense to me. Adolescence is an entire decade of new chemicals and minimal prefrontal cortex support. Really?

No doubt, God has a plan—but it is not clear to me. It certainly involves highly invested, heroic, gracious, Spirit-dependent parents who can fill in the gap. But often, your child will push back, wanting to do it all on their own, lean on their friends, or listen to strangers on social media—convinced they are being reasonable. That's the blind leading the blind.

Where your child was happy to play with friends or a special toy a week ago, now new priorities have emerged. Your child is now all about *enoughness* and *connectedness*.

Enoughness

When children are three or four, they go into the wonderful and maddening question phase. Why? Why? Why?

During adolescence, there is another phase of questioning. Am I good enough? Do my parents love me? Do my friends? Would they like me if they knew the real me? Am I a disappointment? Am I likable? Am I attractive? Am I fun to be with?

Shame, psychologically, begins when children first look into a mirror and realize it is their reflection. But it is during the tween and teen years that they really begin to feel the weight of potentially damaging *measuring* gazes. They begin to feel shame from several sources. Do I fall short of the expectations of the people whom I care about?

Social media is not helpful here. It is gas on the fire. Young adults can now compare themselves, their lives, their likability, their bodies, and their enoughness with others—24/7. But no one wins.[1]

Enoughness is related to the present experience of value and worth in your own eyes and your perception of how others see you.

It turns out this need for enoughness can't be satisfied by the usual suspects: social media, career, family, sexuality choices, sex, taking up good causes, fitness, diet, travel, music, or any other forms of pure busyness.

These things can give you "enoughness hits," but nothing permanent. Jonesing for enoughness is at the root of almost all addictions. If you have mommy or daddy issues, you also have enoughness issues.[2]

Then that nasty critical inner voice shows up. In her book "*Yes, Please,*" comedian Amy Poehler described this inner enemy as a demon voice. She writes:

> This very patient and determined demon shows up in your
> bedroom one day and refuses to leave. You are six or twelve
> or fifteen and you look in the mirror and you hear a voice so

1.   Twenge, Jean M. *iGen: Why Today's Super-Connected Kids Are Growing Up Less Rebellious, More Tolerant, Less Happy—and Completely Unprepared for Adulthood.* Atria Books, 2017; American Psychological Association. *Social Media Use in Adolescence: A Review of the Evidence.* American Psychological Association, 2018.
2.   Bilevicius, Elena, et al. "Shame Mediates the Relationship Between Depression and Addictive Behaviours." *Addictive Behaviors*, vol. 82, 2018, pp. 94–100. DOI: 10.1016/j.addbeh.2018.02.023; Brown, Brené. *Atlas of the Heart: Mapping Meaningful Connection and the Language of Human Experience.* Random House, 2021.

awful and mean that it takes your breath away. It tells you that you are fat and ugly and you don't deserve love. And the scary part is the demon is your own voice.[3]

Dealing with feelings of enoughness often consumes your child.

Connectedness

Connectedness—or, better, the fear of disconnectedness—refers to your child's feelings of being alone, isolated, not in lifegiving relationships, or thinking they are not worthy of loving and being loved, or that they will never feel loved. Disconnectedness is at epidemic proportions today. Disconnectedness and subsequent feelings of loneliness and isolation predispose people to an entire spectrum of mental illnesses, such as:

- depression,
- anxiety,
- suicide ideation,
- incivility, and
- addictive behaviors.

It asks the question, "Can I really count on you? On others?"

You and your teen experience this disconnectedness in the very same place (dACC) in your brain where you experience other pains. So, when you step on a rock, the part of the brain that registers pain in the foot and causes a reactionary, "Ouch!" is the same place where you feel loneliness. Your brain reacts with noticeable tunnel vision until the pain is gone.[4]

---

3. Amy Poehler--Poehler, Amy. *Yes Please*. Dey Street Books, 2014, 214.

4. Eisenberger, Naomi I., Matthew D. Lieberman, and Kipling D. Williams. "Does Rejection Hurt? An fMRI Study of Social Exclusion." *Science*, vol. 302, no. 5643, 2003, pp. 290–292.

When your child feels lonely, their brain is saying "Ouch!" repeatedly. Subconsciously, their brain does what it needs to do to get rid of the pain—including things that may be destructive long term, such as: dangerous relationships, self-medication, and addiction.

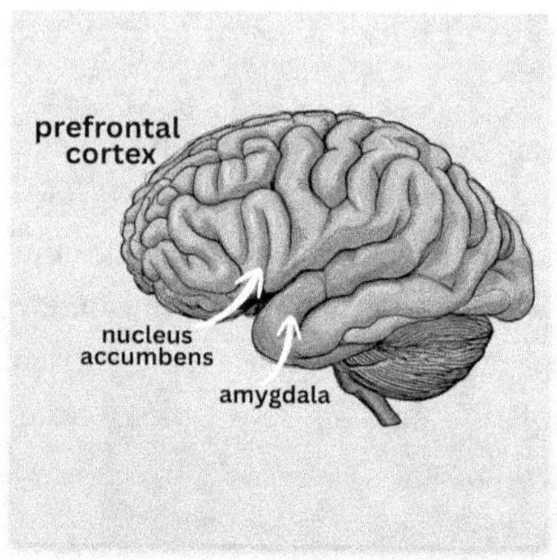

In addition to the constant longings for connectedness and enoughness, there are the new brain toys—hormones and chemicals producing unfamiliar, powerful feelings and desires.

They weren't there last month or last year.

Even at this age, when their prefrontal cortex is still developing, there is a fully formed *nucleus accumbens,* or the "pleasure center," that now liberally releases dopamine when certain actions are performed or substances are ingested. They had brain-dope before, but the amount and speed of delivery are new. This is the foundation of all addictions, whether to drugs, people's opinions of them, or social media.

Tweens and teens are very addiction prone.

There are new sex hormones which, without the prefrontal cortex carburetor, can be very dangerous.

There is the *amygdala* with its cortisol and fear cycles that can lead to more tirades and arguments than last week. Your child might react with fight, flight, or freeze—or just shut down.

With this new chemical cocktail boiling over in their brain, your child will be moodier, more emotional in general, or angrier and more depressed, hungrier and sleepier all at the same time—for little known reason—other than that their brain is unconsciously experimenting with new chemicals and neural pathways that weren't there before.

It is exciting and very confusing.

During this time, as you may have noticed, when you ask, "What is going on with you?" they have no idea.

One anonymous teen tweeted,

I used to not wear make-up. I used to not straighten my hair. I used to not care what anyone thought of me. I used to not care if I didn't have a boyfriend. I used to think that boys were gross. I used to think there was no such thing as "popularity." I used to go for weeks without crying. I used to think everyone was my best friend. I used to love to go to school. I used to be happy all the time. What happened?[5]

Truth is (and GEPs know this), your child is just in the all too human process of becoming the wonderfully talented and unique adult that you've long hoped for—one who can change the world given enough time. But it takes a decade of rapid brain change to get there.

For now, it is not all their fault.

Their brain is a candy store of new and wonderful chemicals.

GEPs know that their child—just like you—desperately needs the Spirit inside them to be the primary source of connectedness and enoughness, particularly during this decade of adolescent change.

---

5. "What Happened?" *Unknown author*. Circulated online image/quote, n.d.

They would benefit from the secrets we learned from Ephesians 3:14-21.

Imagine if they were to ask God for power (in place of the absence of prefrontal cortex power) and begin to feel just how adored they are by God, no matter what they do. In this one relationship at least, they are already enough and connected. Jesus purchased this for them.

If they begin to experience the fullness of God, they won't need filling from others or from addictions as much.

Holy Spirit Make Me Prayer

 I created a "Holy Spirit Make Me" prayer for teens and tweens (bookmarks available on the website gospel-app.com). Check it out. Four prayers. Listen to this first one. Imagine if they were saying this aloud twice a day. It could be noticeable.

"Why Do I Feel This Way?" Prayer

God, I don't feel likable right now. I feel like a failure, and I don't think I'm wanted. I'm not sure how You feel about me, either, God. I keep messing up, and You have very high expectations. I am not even sure that I like myself anymore. So, is it true that You like me as I am? Did Jesus buy that for me? I haven't messed it up? That is the gospel? MAKE ME know that. MAKE ME feel that now, before I go and do something stupid. Make my eyes look up into Yours. Now, please.

To reiterate, their primary source of enoughness and connectedness is God—or should be—just as it is for you. Then they could use you as an important secondary source of enoughness and connectedness. I will show you how—good enough anyway. It won't be easy—but few things are more important for GEPs.

Tip #5

Good Enough Parents Are Aware of the Power of Attunement More Than Non-Good-Enough Parents

*(Your baby needed 30% "in-sync" attunement moments
—your teen still does.)*

Welcome to Tip #5 of GEP. As I've said, parenting is hard. Understanding your child's brain development and how their brain works can be helpful.

Surprisingly, the way your teen or tween handles stress, emotional ups and downs, addictions, anxiety, and relationships of all kinds is foundationally affected by the following:

Nature or Nurture

We used to think that a person's ability to handle stress and emotional triggers was mainly driven by their DNA. We thought they received their sense of enoughness and connectedness from their parents, who received it from theirs.

So little Johnny inherited his sense of independence or proneness to anxiety from his grandfather, through his mother. Some still go that direction, but we no longer believe that it is the biggest influence.

It turns out, your little angel's ability—to play well with others, to handle change and stress, to deal with their swinging emotions during adolescence—now and in the future is largely shaped by early relational attachments formed through attunement with caregivers between the third trimester of pregnancy and age two.[1]

Child development specialists call this specific attachment process *attunement*. Did your infant experience regular attunement moments with a primary caregiver during those early months?

It is in these critical attunement moments—and largely due to them—that infants neurologically develop the ability to:

1) recognize caregivers,

2) learn how to rely on them to keep safe, meet their needs, care for them, help them regulate emotions when stressed, and

3) begin to learn the foundations of what healthy relationships are all about.

These relationships—or their absence—during this critical early development period severely shape how children see the world for decades to come, positively or negatively. Their brains are hardwired during this period, creating an internal working model that shapes their social and emotional lives, heavily influencing how they play with others, how they respond to authority, and their ability to handle stress.

This internal working model begins to develop in their brains long before they are even aware of it. God made us this way. He made us dependent on an "other." As a reminder, my goal at GEP is to become more dependent on God. Infants are emotionally, rela-

---

1. Erikson, Erik. *Childhood and Society*. New York: W. W. Norton & Company, 1950.

tionally, and neurologically dependent upon their parents or guardians.

Attunement

So, what is *attunement*? Per early childhood specialist, Dr. Barbara Sorrels,[2] attunement is:

> The process of a parent feeling the child's feelings, absorbing those feelings, and reflecting them back to the baby, so the baby knows he has been seen, heard and understood. Attunement is more than simply mimicking the child's emotional state; it communicates to the child, "I get you—I understand and empathize with what you're feeling…" A baby is so in-tune with mom that when she holds, rocks, and cuddles her infant, the heartbeat of her baby synchronizes with her own.

**Attunement is as important to the child's growing brain
and emotions as food is to their body.**

Why? Infants are not born with the capacity to regulate their own emotions or deal with distressing events. That area of their brain is not working yet. They are totally reliant upon caregivers for emotional regulation.

Dr. David E. Arredondo explains the power of caregiver-infant attunement during the first year of life.

---

2. Sorrels, Barbara. "Why Parent-Child Attunement Is So Powerful." *Her View From Home*. n.d. Accessed March 26, 2026. https://herviewfromhome.com/why-parent-child-attunement-is-so-powerful/.

This mother and this baby are in a process…a form of reciprocal connectedness called attunement. His eyes and her eyes are locked together—not locked together—but dancing together, really. And in this child's brain a thousand connections per second are being formed and this child is learning to read facial expression. This child is learning about the world. He's learning that the world is responsive or not responsive. He's learning that he can be an object of delight, that he can delight others, he's learning what he's worth. He's learning what the world is like. He's learning so much, so quickly, that we can't even conceive of it.[3]

The caregiver benefits as well. In the caregiver's brain, a variety of chemicals are released that promote ongoing attachment and bonding, including oxytocin (the bonding hormone), dopamine, and other growth-enhancing chemicals.[4] God's little gift to caregivers. Here is a more technical explanation.[5]

Infants do not have the capacity to self-regulate their internal emotional states. Instead, they rely on caregivers to constantly attune to the moment-to-moment shifts in their emotional states. When caregivers respond to an infant's distress, they help to regulate their autonomic nervous

---

3. Arredondo, David. *Attunement: The Key to Empathy.* YouTube video, 7:23. Uploaded by Great Kids Inc., October 7, 2010. Accessed March 22, 2026. https://www.youtube.com/watch?v=IGeS7o4FmRI.

4. "Each moment of such attuned affect facilitates the brain's development and promotes attachment and bonding. Remember, it's in these moments of attunement that both parent and child are most likely to release oxytocin and to feel 'in sync' with one another while also producing growth-enhancing brain chemicals. Attunement builds the relationship by enhancing the functioning of each partner's brain." Baylin, Jonathan, and A. Daniel Hughes. *Brain-Based Parenting: The Neuroscience of Caregiving for Healthy Attachment.* New York: W.W. Norton and Company, 2012.

5. Schore, Allan N. "The Right Brain Is Dominant in Psychotherapy." *Psychotherapy,* vol. 51, no. 3, 2014, pp. 388–397.

system (ANS) by providing a feeling of safety, thereby slowing [their] heartbeat, curving the production of stress hormones and bringing [their] physiology back to a state of calm... As the infant grows older, these mechanisms that were originally controlled by a caregiver gradually become self-regulating.

Psychologist, Dr. Terry Marks-Tarlow writes, "The individual is seen to emerge out of a relationship with a significant other."[6]

This is also true in relation to our ongoing attunement with God through His Spirit. Our spiritual growth, discipleship, and real personality emerge from relational dependence on the key other —God.

We grow less from working harder to be more like Jesus (like we are so often told). No, we grow as we learn to be increasingly *dependent* upon ongoing spiritual attunement. It is the passion of the Spirit to make us feel adored.

But you ask, such *infant* attunement takes a great deal of time and energy that busy young parents, single moms or dads, and working parents can't muster. Are you saying I need to be with my child 24/7?

Good news. Child development specialists suggest that GEPs need to be attuned with their child about 30% of the time. Not 100%, or 90%, or even 50%. Parents of infants can do that—one out of three interactions.

Think of infant attunement as a dance:

Dance Step #1

The child experiences distress or separation.

---

6. Marks-Tarlow, Terry. "The Interpersonal Neurobiology of Clinical Intuition." *Smith College Studies in Social Work* 84, no. 2–2 (2014): 219–236.

Dance Step #2

The primary caregiver co-regulates the child's emotional states using sight, sound, and touch.

Dance Step #3

Emotional synchronicity—the child subconsciously feels a little enoughness and connectedness.

If such good-enough attunement is lacking—and remember, no parent is perfect, nowhere close—the infant's brain won't develop to its full social and emotional potential. That underdevelopment can cause depression, eating disorders, personality disorders, and even suicidal ideation.

What happens in the brain of the misattuned child (the child whose parents were absent, neglectful, or abusive)?

> They stop expressing their need, learn to unconsciously reject their needs and then shut down and disconnect from their needs… Children who experience this sort of deprivation give up their demand for caring and love. They decide unconsciously that there's no hope that their needs will be met. Giving up becomes a common way they respond to stress. As such a child matures, she becomes used to living with these unmet physical and emotional needs. She develops survival strategies, like being really helpful to others and needing very little for herself. She has an unconscious belief that her deepest needs don't matter and that she doesn't matter. She may feel erased and empty, like she doesn't exist. When she risks expressing a need, she gives up easily if someone doesn't respond… When caregivers

consistently attune to a baby's needs, neural networks are built in the brain that support the development of communication and social skills. When there is consistent misattunement, a baby lives in a state of constant stress due to unmet needs creating significant emotional and physiological issues.[7]

Again, this is largely subconscious and not entirely their fault. Because of this, they often come to see the world as unsafe and struggle. They will tend not to trust others, especially adults.

It's brain science. Long before the child is aware, their brain's ability to handle future relationships and emotions is largely hard-wired. It doesn't seem fair, but there it is.[8]

---

7. Gruber, Suzie. "Misattunement—The Invisible ACE." *ACEs Connection*, May 2019. Accessed March 26, 2026. https://www.acesconnection.com/blog/misattune ment-the-invisible-ace?reply=481656068865854097; Harvard University Center on the Developing Child. "Serve and Return." Accessed March 26, 2026. https://develop ingchild.harvard.edu/science/key-concepts/serve-and-return/.
8. Christina Reese, The Wholehearted Child: 10 Ways to Help Kids Live, Love, and Learn Well (Chicago: Moody Publishers, 2018). What are some easy ways that new parents can attune with their infant? Per Christina Reese:
Skin to Skin contact
Eye contact
Intentional play
Peek-a-boo, shaking rattle while gazing into child's eyes
Clapping and smiling when the child does something correctly or something new
Laying on the floor during tummy time and making eye contact.
Mirroring facial expressions
Turn off all external distractions (TV, phone, etc.)
"All of their experiences are 'first time' events that, in turn, create a framework from which they evaluate future events and are, therefore, more impactful. The pathways that are formed in their brains provide the foundation of who they will become. Their personality, and their way of relating to others."

What if you believe that you have already messed it up?

Maybe you are worried that you didn't do 30%. That is one of the reasons I put Tip #1 and #2 ahead of this. In one sense, it doesn't matter how good you were as a parent. None of us was perfect—not even close.

Think of it as a spectrum. Zero is your child wanting to stay in a dark room all day; any slight trigger, and they hyper- or hypo-arouse. Ten is the perfect child, whose primary caregivers were perfect. There was always attunement 24/7. You would agree that is unlikely. Most children are somewhere in the middle.

Let's be honest. Most of us parents weren't aware of attunement. It was not discussed in our mandatory parenting classes. Then life happened: Mom and Dad have a fight or continue fighting. Then there are children #2 through #5. Some families are just trying to survive a pandemic, unemployment, financial worries, putting food on the table, their family's safety, finding a place to live, maybe self-medication is involved, or struggles with their own emotional childhood issues. Maybe it is a single parent who is overwhelmed.

There are generational deficits to consider. Perhaps your parents were absent or abusive. Maybe your caregivers were stressed by day-to-day issues, fighting, or substance abuse. Possibly racism, bullying, or gangs were involved.

As you can see, there are a myriad of real-life issues that will get in the way of perfect attunement. It is not all your fault or your child's. Now what?

First, if you are a Christian, you still have the Holy Spirit in you. God loves you as you are—the parent you are, good enough or not —as much as the Father loves the Son and the Son loves the Father. He can't love you anymore if you were the perfect parent. It is not because of you—*it is all due to the work of Jesus on the cross on your behalf.*

Second, you can ask the Spirit right now (Tip #2) to give you access to God's power so you can begin to feel the height, width, length, and depth of the love of Christ for you (Eph 3). I plead with you to do that.

If you don't know how, go to www.the-dance.org or scan the QR code and complete the free, two-hour intensive, online, virtual spiritual experiential path.

It was created for Christians who feel like they have fallen short and have not lived up to expectations. If you are a parent who feels you are not good enough, it is a must.

Otherwise, that critical voice in your head will hammer you with this new information, shame you, and undermine you moving forward: "See, I've been telling you that you are the problem. You've messed up your child, and there is no way to fix it. Jesus is so disappointed." Your critical inner voice is wrong.

Third, GEPs understand that all is not lost if infancy was less than optimal. It turns out that God divined a second life season when dramatic improvements can be made in your child's brain—a second extended period of potential growth and healing: *adolescence.*

During adolescence, the brains of little Raoul and Maria undergo extensive reorganization, and over half of their neurons are pruned. Which ones? That is dependent partially upon GEPs. Think of adolescence as God's do-over. You are given a mulligan for attunement.

There is great hope for you and your child.

Tip #6

Good Enough Parents Have an Attuning "Gaze" More Than Non-Good-Enough Parents

(Your teen still reads your face like the one-year-old in the "Still Face Experiment.")

Watch the famous *Still Face Experiment* (just two minutes—pause and watch it now).

A mom plays joyfully with her one-year-old… then goes completely blank-faced for two minutes. The baby tries everything—reaching, smiling, crying, screaming—to regain Mom's loving gaze. When it finally returns, the baby collapses in relief.

That experiment wrecks every parent who sees it. Why? Because the baby's entire sense of safety and worth is tied to the mother's gaze.

It's not that the mother wasn't there—she was physically present. What mattered was *attunement*: the baby became insecure when she looked at her mother's face and didn't feel loved, acknowledged, attached, appreciated, connected, or attuned—you pick the word.

Even though the mother was there, the infant still felt abandoned, exposed, distressed, alone, afraid, not enough, and not connected to her source of comfort, meaning, identity, and worth.

Her mother's attuned gaze provided her with an immediate sense of identity and security. She could only see herself reflected in her mother's eyes. Does that make sense? Even though she couldn't process it, her brain was subconsciously asking, "Can I count on you?" and "Am I worthy of being loved?"—questions of connectedness and enoughness.

God created all of us this way. It's a brain thing. We still experience it. We are subconsciously asking the same questions.

Here's the uncomfortable truth: your teenager reads your face the same way, just more subtly. Please don't miss this, GEP. Even now, your child desperately needs to see your love and approval in your gaze. When your teen enters a room with you in it, they desperately need to hear, see, and feel you adoring them—to see it in your face, your eyes, your body language, your words—just like the mother in the *Still Face* video—adapted for teens.

Their brain is screaming for a sense of enoughness and connectedness from anyone and everyone, but especially from you. Their brain, 24/7, is asking the two questions of both you and God. "Can I count on you?" and "Am I worthy of being loved?"

When they walk into the room, their brain is constantly scanning:

- Do your eyes light up?
- Does your face soften with delight?
- Or is it "still faced"—disappointment, frustration, exhaustion?

Even if they act like they don't care, their midbrain is screaming the same two questions the baby's brain asked.

This mirrors how the Bible describes our relationship with God. There is a Hebrew idiom, *lipne Elohim,* meaning "in the presence of God," or literally, "in front of God's face." Our relationship with God echoes this longing to see God's delight reflected back to us, like a version of the *Still Face Experiment.*

I will be honest. I do not wake up feeling that God loves me—that if I were to look into his face, I would see enthusiasm and joy. I *know* that is the case, but I often *feel* more like the infant when the mother goes "still faced." I am shame-prone and riddled with insecurities. But I want to experience God's face alive and shining when He looks into my eyes.

This is Biblical. Israel longed for that—it was critical to their whole identity. Check out these verses.

"May God be gracious to us and bless us and make his face shine upon us, Selah." (Psalm 67:1)

"Do not hide your face from me, do not turn your servant away in anger… Do not reject me or forsake me, O God my Savior." (Psalm 27:9)

"Tell Aaron and his sons, 'This is how you are to bless the Israelites. Say to them: The Lord bless you and keep you; the Lord make his face shine upon you and be gracious to you; the Lord turn his face toward you and give you peace.'" (Numbers 6:23-26)

If you are not regularly experiencing God's smiling face—or haven't felt it recently—you might feel like an adult version of the one-year-old in the *Still Face* video. You might spiritually twitch and shriek and cry out or do things—often reactionary things—to feel God smiling on you again. Your brain is subconsciously asking the same questions about God that the child's brain was asking: "Can I count on you?" and "Am I worthy of your love?"

Then there are those other moments when, by faith, we look up and see God smiling, dancing, laughing, and we are spiritually secure again. We dance again, too. We feel shalom again. Heaven will be filled with that. It is joy.

Your teen desperately needs to see God's delight in your eyes—you're the closest representation of God that they interact with daily.

Ask the Spirit (Ephesians 3) to sync your heart with the Father's heart until you feel His crazy love for your child—exactly as they are today. Then let that love leak out in your gaze, your tone, your hug.

It won't fix everything, but it will be the single most healing thing you can offer during the adolescent remodel. I promise you, when God looks down at your Christian child, your son or daughter, He is saying, "You are my beloved child with whom I am well pleased. I have your back. Look up into my eyes and see. Yes, you can count on me. Yes, you are worthy of my love."

Tip #7

Good Enough Parents Are More Aware of Their Child's Attachment Style Than Non-Good-Enough Parents (Part 1)

(There are four quadrants—only one is secure.)

I can't tell you how important this is to parenting. In this tip and the next, I will set the table, and the rest of the meal will follow.

Will these two tips fix your teen? What does that even mean? They will help you see that it is not *all* your child's fault—or yours.

They provide doable objectives to help your child experience a more secure attachment style and begin to answer the key core questions: "Can I count on you?" and "Am I worthy of being loved?" In other words: connectedness and enoughness.

First, a little psychology—don't worry, you won't get lost in the weeds. I am not trying to make you a neuroscientist.

We dabbled in attachment theory when I discussed infant and adolescent attunement.

Let's drill deeper.

Attachment theory holds that all humanity is foundationally relational. Men and women are innately *Homo vinculum* beings—those who bond. That is one of the unique core things about us.

Counselor Susan Johnson, in her book on attachment theory, says:

"We are first and foremost a social, relational and bonding species. Over the lifespan, the need for connection with others shapes our neural architecture, our responses to stress, our everyday emotional lives, and the interpersonal dramas and dilemmas that are at the heart of those lives."[1]

Author and speaker Brené Brown concurs:

"What comes from the inside of us is a very human need to belong, to relate. We are wired for connection. It's in our biology... Connection is critical because we all have the basic need to feel accepted and to believe that we belong and are valued for who we are."[2]

We get this honestly. Biblically, we reflect the Trinitarian community—God's image and likeness.

This truth is beyond my understanding, but it certainly includes our need for emotional and relational bonding.

God is and has always been innately connected and constantly engaging. This attachment is more than people hanging out in the same vicinity. It includes a healthy, felt sense of connection.

This is one of the reasons I chose the theme of the Trinity for the free online experience, *The Dance* (www.the-dance.org). It is an online gospel journey for people who are struggling with enoughness.

Remember, our need and desire for such dynamic, safe attach-

---

1.   Johnson, Susan M. *Attachment Theory in Practice: Emotionally Focused Therapy (EFT) with Individuals, Couples, and Families*. New York: Guilford Press, 2019.
2.   Brown, Brené. *Braving the Wilderness: The Quest for True Belonging and the Courage to Stand Alone*. New York: Random House, 2017.

ment begins in infancy, when infants learn to attach emotionally and physically to adults who are responsive to their needs—a process called *attunement.*

These early attachment relationships develop into the brain's inner working models that become the child's framework for viewing and understanding the world, others, and themselves for decades to come.

From infancy and onward, our need for this *attachment* is as strong as our need for food.

This attachment is more than just *being there.* The quality and power of the attachment bond is a function of three things: the perceived accessibility, responsiveness, and emotional engagement of important others—those who are our primary caregivers.

These three provide the child with the answer to their subjective, and so often subconscious, worry: "Are you there for me?"

Infants are born totally dependent upon this deep form of attachment with *others.*[3]

The infant's midbrain begins to relax as they come to know that their caregiver is caring and dependable—in a word—secure.

Or the opposite. An insecure base hardwires the child's developing brain to feel not-enoughness and disconnectedness, making them hesitant to explore their world—in a word—insecure.

In either case, during the first two years of life, the infant's brain becomes hardwired with an *internal working model* of present and expected enoughness and connectedness that shapes their lives for years—even decades to come.

This is their *attachment style.*

You may ask, "What if the early attachment experience of my

---

3. Ainsworth, Mary D. S., Mary C. Blehar, Everett Waters, and Sally Wall. Patterns of Attachment. Hillsdale, NJ: Lawrence Erlbaum Associates, 1978; Bowlby, John. Attachment and Loss. Vol. 1: Attachment. New York: Basic Books, 1969; Erikson, Erik H. Childhood and Society. New York: W. W. Norton & Company, 1950; Siegel, Daniel J. The Developing Mind. New York: Guilford Press, 1999.

child was sketchy?" Don't worry. GEPs know there is a second life season for a redo—adolescence. GEPs step up their game during adolescence.

That's why you are reading this book.

Four Attachment Quadrants

Consider the attachment style diagram on the next page. The vertical axis (y-axis)—the connectedness axis—is your child's expectation and experience of positive connectedness (higher on the axis) or fears of unhealthy connectedness (lower on the axis).

In other words, "Do I look to relationships for my sense of worth and security or not?"

Or even more simply, "Can I count on you?"

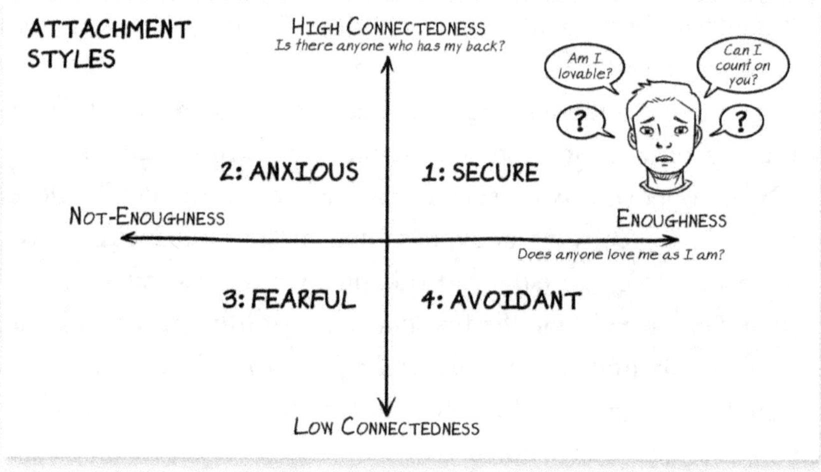

The horizontal axis (x-axis) is your child's inner sense of enoughness. A positive sense of enoughness (to the right on the axis) reflects a healthy self-regard that does not require much external validation from others, social media, or success.

This spectrum answers their unspoken question, "Am I worthy of your love?"

The two axes form four quadrants of attachment styles: Going counterclockwise from the upper right quadrant, they are: secure, anxious, fearful and avoidant—one secure and three insecure.

In this tip, I will explore the secure attachment style in Quadrant #1.

Secure Attachment

From the *Still Face Experiment*, the one-year-old toddler experienced immediate distress when her mother's gaze disappeared. That makes sense. But when her mother's caring gaze returned, she was immediately comforted.

She is a *secure* child.

The secure child's subconscious wiring reflects a strong sense of self-worth, along with the expectation that others are generally accepting and responsive: in other words, a healthy sense of enoughness and connectedness.

To the internal question, "Can I count on you?" their inner working model will tend to answer, "Yes!"

To the internal question, "Am I worthy of your love?" the unspoken answer is, "Yes!"

As they grow older, secure children tend to make friends quickly and play well with others.

They are comfortable with closeness and their need for others.

They also tend to deal well with emotional distress.

Listen to this descriptor and see if it fits your child.

It is relatively easy for me to become emotionally close to others. I am comfortable depending on others and having others depend on me. I don't worry about being alone or having others not accept me.[4]

---

4. Adapted from Kim Bartholomew and Leonard M. Horowitz, "Attachment Styles

According to Mikulincer and Shaver, who conducted research on attachment theory applied to adults, secure attachment has been linked "to almost every positive index of mental health and general well-being outlined in the social sciences:"[5]

- resilience in the face of stress,
- optimism,
- high self-esteem,
- curiosity,
- the ability to self-disclose and be assertive,
- tolerate ambiguity,
- regulate difficult emotions,
- grasp and tolerate different perspectives,
- empathy,
- compassion,
- openness to people perceived as different from oneself,
- and a tendency to altruistic action.

Secure children can explore their environment more freely than insecure children.

They tend to trust that their parents and other adults will support them in their natural explorations of the world.

As they mature, they seem more resilient and better able to handle the ups and downs of relationships and the world in general, largely because they can effectively regulate their emotions.

If this is your child, don't mess it up. Dance a little.

I will cover the three *insecure* quadrants in the next tip. For now, I have an exercise for you.

---

among Young Adults: A Test of a Four-Category Model," *Journal of Personality and Social Psychology* 61, no. 2 (1991): 226–244, https://doi.org/10.1037/0022-3514.61.2.226.

5. Mikulincer, Mario, and Phillip Shaver. *Attachment in Adulthood: Structure, Dynamics, and Change*. 2nd ed. New York: Guilford Press, 2016.

My Teen's Attachment Style Survey

On the next page, is the "My Teen's Attachment Style Survey." It is a Likert scale with 16 items.

For each statement, choose one of the following: strongly agree, agree, feel neutral, disagree, or strongly disagree.

Obviously, this is from your point of view—but it is a good place to start.

Why do GEPs want to know their child's attachment style?

One, it helps you see that your child's actions, reactions, and responses are not *all* your child's fault—or yours.

Secondly, it may help shape your immediate response.

What do I mean?

If your child is in one of the three insecure quadrants, and they trigger, react badly, lie, blow a fuse, dysregulate, or storm out of the room in rage, it may not be helpful for you to try to reason with them or even discipline them in that moment.

It may only make them feel more insecure, trigger again, feel more not-enoughness and disconnectedness—and cycle to the lower right in the "Gospel App Shape" (illustrated in Tip #2).

So many existing how-to parenting books fail in this area. Their instructions can work well with secure children but can be extremely shaming to insecure ones.

So far, we have only considered the secure quadrant.

I will get to the other three in the next tip.

Remember, there is no right or wrong quadrant. It doesn't make one child better and another worse, or one parent more *good enough* than another. Honestly, it is what it is. Remember, your child's attachment style is likely well-rooted and somewhat hardwired, but not completely. Particularly during adolescence, it is more fluid.

My Teen's Attachment Style Survey

	Strongly Agree 5	Agree 4	Neutral 3	Disagree 2	Strongly Disagree 1
1. I am comfortable without close emotional relationships.	5	4	3	2	1
2. I want to be completely intimate with others.	5	4	3	2	1
3. It is relatively easy for me to become emotionally close to others.	5	4	3	2	1
4. Others seem generally impersonal and distant to me.	5	4	3	2	1
5. I am somewhat uncomfortable getting close to others.	5	4	3	2	1
6. I want to be emotionally close to others but find it difficult to trust others.	5	4	3	2	1
7. I am uncomfortable being without close relationships.	5	4	3	2	1
8. I am comfortable depending on others and having them depend upon me.	5	4	3	2	1
9. It is important for me to feel independent and self-sufficient.	5	4	3	2	1
10. I often find that others are reluctant to get as close as I would like.	5	4	3	2	1
11. I sometimes worry that I will be hurt if I become too close to others.	5	4	3	2	1
12. I prefer not to depend on others or have them depend upon me.	5	4	3	2	1
13. I don't worry about being alone.	5	4	3	2	1
14. I find it difficult to depend upon others.	5	4	3	2	1
15. I sometimes worry that others don't value me as much as I value them.	5	4	3	2	1
16. I feel that others generally accept me.	5	4	3	2	1

Calculations for My Teen's Attachment Style Survey

(The highest result reflects your assessment of your teen's attachment style)

_________ Secure (Add Q3+Q8+Q13+Q16)

_________ Avoidant (Add Q1+Q9+Q12+Q4)

_________ Anxious (Add Q2+Q10+Q7+Q15)

_________ Fearful (Add Q5+Q6+Q14+Q11)

. . .

Parent, keep this in mind. Strictly because of what Jesus did for your Christian child 2000 years ago, God loves your child as much as the Father loves the Son and the Spirit and the Son and the Spirit love the Father. Jesus loves secure and insecure children the same. He alone has the power to ultimately make the insecure feel more secure—to make them experience more enoughness and more connectedness. This is the wheelhouse of the Spirit.

The next tip will show you how that can work.

Tip #8

Good Enough Parents Are More Aware of Their Child's Attachment Style Than Non-Good-Enough Parents (Part 2)

Let's review. We started by learning how the *Simple Uncluttered Gospel* can make a difference in your relationship with your child and in their sense of self and security. Bottom line—there is power available that can change things. Reminder: Repeat the *SUG* twice a day.

We discussed the latest and greatest in neuroscience and talked about the differences between adult and teen brains. The difficulties are not all your teen's fault—or yours.

We then shifted to attachment theory, in particular, the importance of attunement in infants and adolescents.

Lastly, we looked at the secure attachment style and the importance of understanding your teen better.

In this tip, I will explore how you can recognize the three insecure attachment styles in your teen, perhaps by reviewing the "My Teen's Attachment Style Survey" and observing their behaviors and responses. This awareness can help you tailor your approach to foster security.

Insecure Attachments

The three types of insecure attachment styles are: Anxious, Fearful, and Avoidant.[1]

Attachment insecurities are associated with vulnerability to depression, anxiety disorders (PTSD, OCD, and GAD), personality disorders (i.e., borderline personality disorder, schizoid and avoidant personality disorders), conduct disorders, antisocial tendencies, and addiction.

Watch this video of what scientists refer to as the "Strange Experiment." These two children are "insecure." In both cases, their moms left them alone—tears, more tears. That makes sense. Note how the children treat their mom when she returns.

Insecure Child Quadrant 4: Avoidant

In the "Strange Experiment" clip, when his mother returns, the insecure, avoidant child "avoids" her—at least her eyes.

Even though he wants his mother's comfort, his inner working model of insecurity will subconsciously put up boundaries, even when she is holding him.

Why? Likely, when he was distressed in the past, he felt that his caregiver ignored him or that he had become an annoyance. He has learned subconsciously not to seek comfort from her. He won't even look into his mother's gaze, perhaps afraid of what he might see— or not see.

The avoidant child generally has a positive sense of self-worth

1. Kim Bartholomew and Leonard M. Horowitz, "Attachment Styles among Young Adults: A Test of a Four-Category Model," *Journal of Personality and Social Psychology* 61, no. 2 (1991): 226–244.

or enoughness—meaning that they can do things on their own. But they lack the expectation that relationships will benefit them.

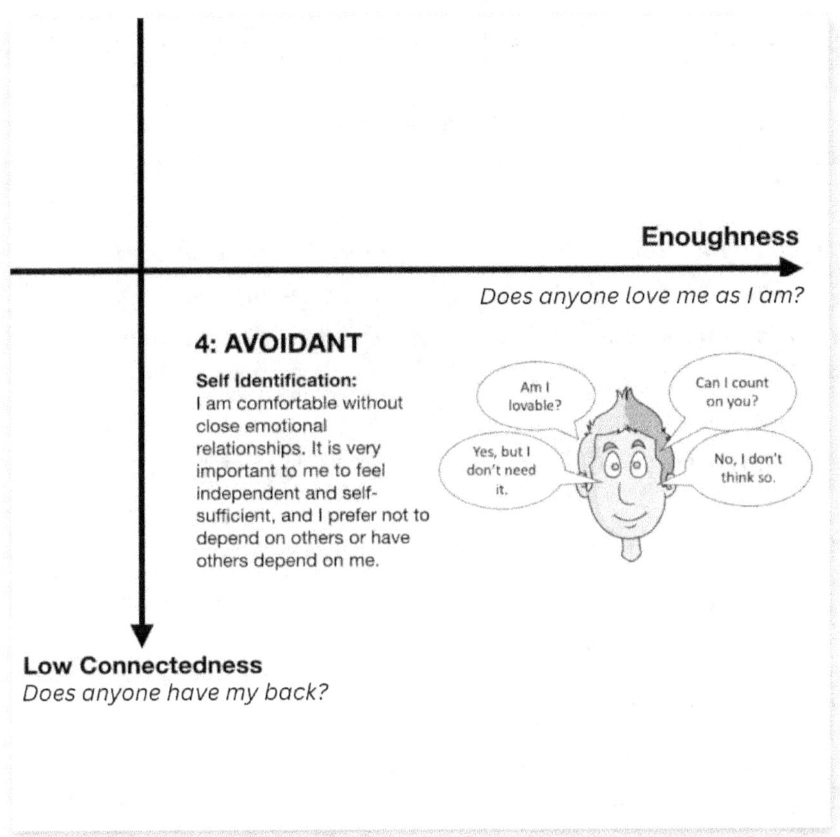

All other things equal, they prefer less drama and tend to be more withdrawn and, typically, will avoid or be somewhat suspicious of emotional closeness.

In times of distress, they have some difficulty accepting comfort from their caregivers. Their brain will shift to an avoidance strategy. Avoidants struggle to be empathetic and are less willing to take responsibility for others' welfare or to offer help.

To be clear, this child is not broken. He is very human, given the cards he has been dealt.

Can he live a fulfilled life? Can he become more trusting? More empathetic? More secure?

Of course.

Remember, the GEP sees adolescence as a time for a special re-do.

Teens in this quadrant would resonate with the following descriptor.

I am comfortable without close emotional relationships. It is very important to me to feel independent and self-sufficient, and I prefer not to depend on others or have others depend on me.[2]

To the core questions:

"Am I worthy of your love?" They might answer, "Yes, but I don't need it."

"Can I count on you?" They might answer, "No, I don't think so."

Insecure Child Quadrant #2: Anxious

The anxious child, like the second child in the clip, reacts subconsciously to his mother's return with exaggerated displays of distress and anger.

He even *punishes* the mother by slapping the toy away.

Why? This *fight* response is designed to protest distance and get an attachment figure to pay more attention.

Anxious teens tend to feel a lower sense of self-worth or enoughness—and generally try to fill that gap with attachments to key *others*, seeking connectedness—in whose measuring gazes they expect to feel adored and wanted.

This is mostly subconscious.

---

2. Adapted from Bartholomew and Horowitz, "Attachment Styles," 226–244.

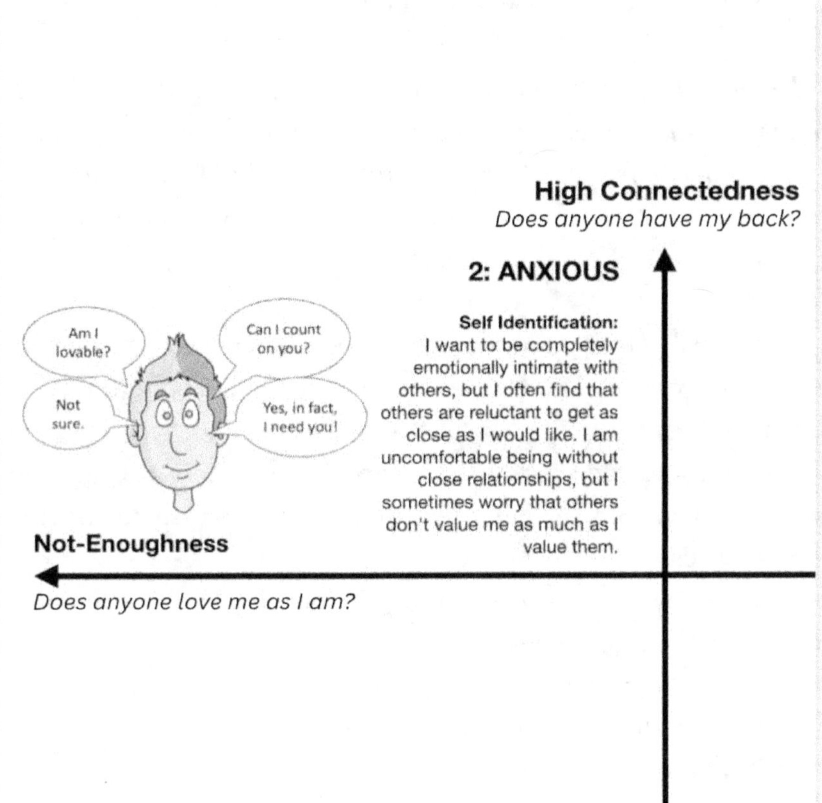

The *others* may be friends or social media followers.

They can be emotionally co-dependent and even grabby in relationships—and will likely be triggered if they feel left out, don't know the inside jokes, feel betrayed or abandoned.

Their inner voice tells them they need others to make them feel better about themselves.

They would agree with the following:

I want to be completely emotionally intimate with others. Still, I often find that others are reluctant to get as close as I would like. I am uncomfortable being without close relationships, but I sometimes worry that others don't value me as much as I value them.[3]

Anxiously attached people tend to be self-focused—preoccupied with their own distress. Or they might offer care that does not meet the others' needs.

Anxious people seem to feel empathy outwardly but inevitably become caught up in their own distress rather than tuning in to others' needs.

Subconsciously, they will use relationships and community to feel better about themselves.

To the core questions:

"Am I worthy of your love?" "Not sure."

"Can I count on you?" "Yes, in fact, I need you."

Insecure Child Quadrant #3: Fearful

The fearful child combines a subconscious sense of not-enoughness with fear of disconnectedness—the worst of both worlds.

Their brain's inner working model subconsciously leads them to avoid vulnerability and openness out of fear of possible rejection.

This person often vacillates between longing and fear, demanding connection and then pulling away and even attacking when connection is offered.

It can be called disorganized attachment in children.

---

3. Adapted from Bartholomew and Horowitz, "Attachment Styles," 226–244.

They would agree with the following:

I am somewhat uncomfortable getting close to others. I want emotionally close relationships, but I find it difficult to trust others completely or to depend on them. I sometimes worry that I will be hurt if I allow myself to become too close to others.[4]

Children with some history of trauma, abuse, and neglect can typically present fearful tendencies. These children may seek their parents' attention with intensity, then try to avoid them with equal intensity out of fear.

They vacillate between highly anxious and highly avoidant strategies.

They may blow up or shut down emotionally.

To the core questions:

"Am I worthy of your love?" "I do not think so."

"Can I count on you?" "I want to, but no, it's too risky."

Review

Most teens bounce between two insecure quadrants, but one usually dominates:

Quadrant 2 – Anxious

- Clings, people-pleases, and explodes when they sense rejection
- Constantly seeks reassurance: "Do you still love me?"
- Social media obsession, dramatic breakups, fear of abandonment
- Underlying subconscious belief: "I'm not enough unless people prove I am."

---

4. Adapted from Bartholomew and Horowitz, "Attachment Styles," 226–244.

Quadrant 3 – Fearful

- Chaos: hot/cold, push/pull, self-sabotage
- History of trauma, neglect, or wildly inconsistent parenting
- Trusts no one fully, including themselves
- Underlying subconscious belief: "The world is unsafe, and I'm broken anyway."

Quadrant 4 – Avoidant

- "I'm fine," walls up, mocks vulnerability
- Minimizes emotions, ghosts friends, claims they don't need anyone
- Underlying subconscious belief: "Depending on people is weakness and risky; I can do this alone."

Quadrant 1 – Secure (the goal)

- Can self-soothe and reach out when needed
- Handles conflict without panic or shutting down
- Knows they're loved even when they mess up

Good Enough Parents don't diagnose in order to shame—they diagnose in order to understand.

When your teen storms out, ghosts you for three days, or melts down over a text, ask: "Which quadrant is this behavior coming from today?"

Then respond with the one thing that moves every insecure quadrant toward secure: consistent, felt, adolescent-appropriate attunement. More on exactly how in the following tips.

GEPs, remember to keep saying the *SUG* aloud twice a day. Keep that going. You will be surprised by the difference it can make, and anyone can do it.

Tip #9

Good Enough Parents Teach and Model for Their Teens How to Preach the Gospel to Themselves

In the last couple of tips, I introduced an *Attachment Styles* diagram to help GEPs see how their teen's attachment style influences their behavior and relationships. I invited GEPs to determine which quadrant best reflects their teen's current attachment style. Hopefully, you have learned something new about your child.

Teens who tend to exhibit any of the three insecure attachments —between 30 and 50% of teens, and up to 70% in high-risk contexts—will struggle with relationships, with authority, with addiction, and with self-worth. It is not all their fault; much of it operates at a subconscious level. They can't just choose to stop it. I believe they subconsciously want answers to the two core questions:

1) "Am I worthy of your love?" and
2) "Can I count on you?"

But their midbrain betrays them. This is normal post-fall humanity.

Where do they look for a sense of enoughness and connectedness? Wherever and whenever they can—friends, social media, appearance, compliments, sex, pornography, eating disorders, identity struggles, sexuality issues, self-medication, addictions, self-destructive habits like cutting, lying, and even religious activities they believe might add connectedness and enoughness with God—some good things, some sketchy.

This longing is not under the management of their prefrontal cortex. They are not being reasonable, so trying to reason them into Quadrant #1 has almost zero chance of working. Stop trying.

GEPs have a better understanding that their teens are *not* mini-me's, little logical reflections of the parents who should be expected to be reasonable. Remember, their prefrontal cortex is still under construction.

Here's Brené Brown speaking about all of us, but this applies to our teens:

The constant struggle to feel accepted and worthy is unrelenting. We put so much of our time and energy into making sure that we meet everyone's expectations and into caring about what other people think of us, that we are often left feeling angry, resentful and fearful. Sometimes we turn these emotions inward and convince ourselves that we are bad and that maybe we deserve the rejection that we so desperately fear. Other times we lash out—we scream at our partners and children for no apparent reason, or we make a cutting comment to a friend or colleague. Either way, in the end, we are left feeling exhausted, overwhelmed and alone.[1]

Does this sound familiar? It's what real people in Quadrants #2 through #4 experience. I am not trying to cast shade on your teen. I

---

1. Brené Brown, *I Thought It Was Just Me (but It Isn't): Telling the Truth About Perfectionism, Inadequacy, and Power* (New York: Gotham Books, 2007), 20.

struggle too! It does not mean your children are good or bad, right or wrong. They are imperfect humans in an imperfect world.

Like someone said, "Heaven will be great, this ain't it."

GEPs remember that strictly because of what Jesus has done, God loves their child as they are, not as they should be. Jesus came for insecure children and adults.

Ultimately, that is all there is.

The Spirit in your child's inner being not only has the power, but the motivation to make them–MAKE them–feel more loved, more enough, and more connected.

Recall from the last tip that GEPs understand their teenager will be affected by their attachment style inner working model until they die. They won't die from it, but with it.

This is what separates GEPs from NGEPs. GEPs know their teen's attachment style *can* shift toward Quadrant #1, particularly during adolescence.

Not perfectly, that's Heaven, but noticeably.

Think of a spectrum from zero to ten. Ten is a perfectly secure child—there has only been one: Jesus.

For whatever reason, let's say your child entered adolescence at a two, GEPs know how to help them evolve to a four or a six. Still not a ten—that's Heaven.

But a six is a 200% improvement in relational security, a sense of enoughness, the ability to enter relationships vulnerably, and overall satisfaction and joy.

They will need others less.

They will need social media less.

The keyword is *need*. Your teenager will eventually thank you —likely when they are 30 or so—but maybe, just maybe, sooner.

How do GEPs do it? That's what I want to talk about over the next few tips.

First things first. GEPs know the power of the gospel to reach their teen's powerful, subconscious mid-brain and begin to fill their cup with the mysterious fullness of God (Eph 3:14-21).

This is the GEP's goal this side of Heaven, to make sure and do whatever they can—directly or indirectly—to regularly expose and immerse their teen in the message of the *Simple Uncluttered Gospel.*

Check out the following four gospel prayers for teens. I have them on a single bookmark prayer card available on the website (www.gospel-app.com) .

It is wise to get them into your teens' hands, voices, and heads. Youth pastors can use them in groups, in opening prayers, in newsletters, and in podcasts. This is an immersion strategy—quickly implemented.

If you start them doing this pre-adolescence, you won't regret it. Using these "Holy Spirit Make Me" prayers equips your teen to:

1) admit that they can't make it happen,

2) ask God to intervene miraculously, and

3) be a missionary to their own critical inner voice.

Frankly, we would all benefit from doing this. It would make a noticeable difference.

Imagine your teen saying these prayers twice daily—aloud (that is important). The Holy Spirit's passion—His secret mission—is to make your teen feel more enoughness and connectedness related to Him.

"Why Do I Feel This Way?" Prayer

God, I don't feel likable right now. I feel like a failure, and I don't think I'm wanted. I'm not sure how You feel about me either. God, I keep messing up, and You have very high expectations. I am not even sure that I like myself anymore. So, is it true that You like me as I am? Did Jesus buy that for me? I haven't messed it up? That is the gospel? MAKE ME know that. MAKE ME feel that now, before I go and do something stupid. Make my eyes look up into Yours. Now please.

"What's Wrong with Me?" Prayer

God, I am ashamed, and I feel like everything I do is messed up. What is wrong with me? You should be wildly disappointed in me. But, 2000 years ago, You poured out Your anger, disappointment, and criticism on Jesus, Your own Son, instead of me. So now, You can't be disappointed in me, ever. MAKE ME really get that.

Jesus' record of doing everything right is now, for some crazy reason, put into my story, including everything His life earned. Now, You love AND like me as much as You love and like Jesus. That is more than ANYONE else loves and likes me. It might feel like You are disappointed in me, but that is NEVER true.

Give me power to believe that You love *and* like me. Holy Spirit, give me Your power to defeat the inner critical voice in my head that spews shame, guilt, and fear. When I mess up again, MAKE ME feel loved by You. MAKE ME see Your smile and hear your voice. Now please.

"What Do You Think of Me?" Prayer

God, I am kind of afraid of You sometimes. I want to look up and see into Your eyes, but I am also scared of what I might see. I need Your power to MAKE ME want to look up. To be honest, I wonder if You could ever be proud of me. I want You to be. I want to believe that You are. I know that Jesus purchased that for me, I just have a hard time believing it in my soul. Holy Spirit, MAKE ME believe it is true. I need to know that You love me as I am. Sometimes people treat me so poorly, but You say that I am honored. I am tired of trying so hard to be good enough. Spirit, quick, give me power to look up and see Your adoring eyes toward me now. (Gal 4:4-7)

"What Do You Have for Me?" Prayer

Jesus, I am back. I did it again, the very thing that I promised I wouldn't do. What's wrong with me? I couldn't help it. I am ashamed, tired and afraid. I need to ask, Jesus, did You die for that choice of mine? You did? It is paid for? Completely? Holy Spirit, MAKE ME believe that, now.

I have another question. If I were to look up into Your eyes right now, would I see that You really like me as I am, even though I keep running to the same destructive thing instead of You? You know that I will probably disappoint You again and again? MAKE ME look up and see You loving me, no matter what. That is the gospel, right? MAKE ME understand that now. Give me power to look up and MAKE ME want to run to You a little bit more than before.

As your teen says these prayers and they take root in their midbrain, your teen will begin to develop a new habit that will compete with the very entrenched, powerful, and insecure midbrain.

I understand they will not resonate with every prayer, every day. But they are creating a new habit of dependence upon God as their prime source of enoughness and connectedness.

During adolescence, your child's brain is undergoing a massive overhaul: billions of new neurons are added daily, while old, unused neurons are pruned. The brain is in a use-it-or-lose-it mode.

Now is a strategically perfect time to activate their gospel self-preaching neurons.

Let me elaborate a bit. Suppose your teen tends toward Quadrant #2, anxious. They struggle with a lack of a sense of enoughness and seek validation from others.

But what if the Holy Spirit mysteriously MAKES your child feel a little more connected to the trinitarian Father, Son, and Spirit? They might experience a noticeable shift toward the security of Quadrant #1. They will need the measuring gaze of others less. GEPs will celebrate that.

What if they are in Quadrant #4, avoidant? For so many reasons, they have come to learn that relationships are fragile and often disappointing. So, they prefer to trust themselves—loneliness is better than being hurt.

But what if the Holy Spirit, in their inner being, MAKES them feel more connected and they begin to experience how wonderful their vertical relationship with God truly is? If their fears of relationships are cast out a little by God's perfect love (1 John 4:18), maybe they can begin to trust others more.

What if they were in Quadrant #3, fearful? They tend to have a low sense of enoughness and fear of connectedness. But what if the Holy Spirit in their inner being begins to make them hear and believe God saying to them, "You are my beloved child, with whom I am well pleased."

What if the Spirit immerses them in the perfect love that casts out fear? (1 John 4:13) Can you imagine the difference—not perfectly, that's for Heaven, but feeling a little more secure, leaning toward Quadrant #1.

GEPs know that if their teen develops a habit of running to God for filling when they feel a lack of enoughness or connectedness, good things can happen. The *Simple Uncluttered Gospel,* in the hands of the Holy Spirit in your teens' inner being (Eph 3:14-21), is *that* powerful—more powerful than their entrenched critical inner voice. GEPs dance a little.

I have mentioned it before, if you would like more information on this topic, check out the online experiential path, *The Dance (the-dance.org).* In as little as two hours, you and your teen will get a crash course on the passion of the Spirit to make us feel attached to God—beginning right away.

Tip #10

Good Enough Parents Are More Aware of Their Own Attachment Styles Than Non-Good-Enough Parents

(Your teen doesn't need a parent to rescue them
—they need a safe and trusted person who gets it.)

Not only are GEPs a little more aware of their teen's and tween's attachment style, but they:

1) more clearly understand that it is not all their fault.

2) have a starting point for becoming more intentional and strategic in loving others.

GEPs are also more aware of their own attachment styles. (You didn't think that I would let you get through this unscathed, did you?)

Remember, no shame here at GEP. In the end, I want spiritually dancing parents.

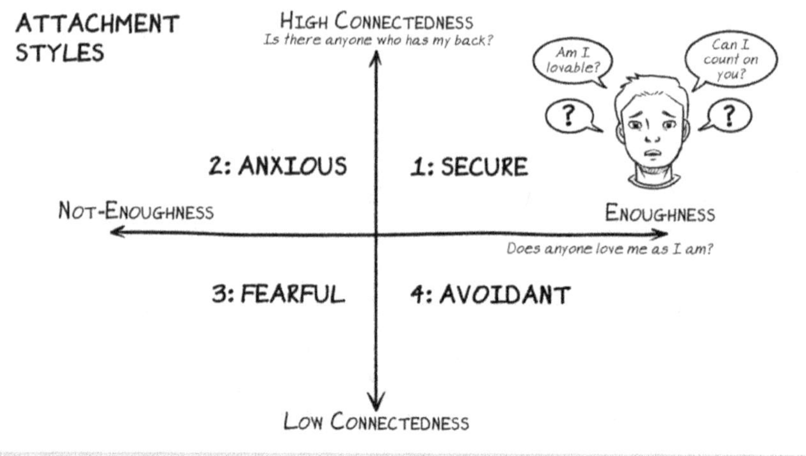

Here is the attachment style diagram again—a few things to consider as we proceed.

If you're feeling overwhelmed or unsure where to begin, remember that understanding is a process, and small steps can lead to meaningful change.

- Breathe. No one is perfectly or totally any one style. Think of a spectrum from zero to ten. No one is at the extreme ends; we are all somewhere in the middle.
- No quadrant is right or better than the other quadrants. If you self-identify as being in one of the three insecure quadrants, this does not mean that you are broken or evil —but you do have impediments to experiencing enoughness and connectedness—and to one degree or another, you will tend to use your child to satisfy those needs subconsciously. Remember, many parents face similar challenges. You are not alone in this journey.
- Strictly because of what Jesus did for you 2000 years ago, God loves you as much as the Father loves the Son and the Spirit and vice versa. God loves insecure teens *and* parents. He is crazy about you, whether you are

secure, avoidant, fearful, or anxious. He adores Non-GEPs as much as GEPs. He is proud to dance with you.

- Reminder: there is no such thing as a perfectly secure parent. Period. All of us are to one degree or another insecure. It is not all our fault. But there is something we can do.

Keep saying the *SUG* twice a day, until you notice a difference —or better, until your teen notices a difference.

The Good Enough Parent Attachment Style Survey

On the next page is the "Good Enough Parent Attachment Style Survey," a 16-item Likert scale.

For each statement, do you strongly agree, agree, feel neutral, disagree, or strongly disagree?

Take the survey to identify your tendencies and gain insight into your attachment style.

I have discussed extensively what characterizes insecure teens.

Now let's investigate what characterizes insecure parents.

Recognizing attachment styles can help you feel more hopeful and empowered to improve family dynamics. So many conflicts are related to attachment styles—and as always, "it takes two to tango."

Understanding these dynamics can reassure you that change is possible.

Following the survey are general descriptions of each attachment style. Notice which ones resonate with you.

Dr. Bill Senyard

Good Enough Parent's Attachment Style Survey

	Strongly Agree 5	Agree 4	Neutral 3	Disagree 2	Strongly Disagree 1
1. I am comfortable without close emotional relationships.	5	4	3	2	1
2. I want to be completely intimate with others.	5	4	3	2	1
3. It is relatively easy for me to become emotionally close to others.	5	4	3	2	1
4. Others seem generally impersonal and distant to me.	5	4	3	2	1
5. I am somewhat uncomfortable getting close to others.	5	4	3	2	1
6. I want to be emotionally close to others but find it difficult to trust others.	5	4	3	2	1
7. I am uncomfortable being without close relationships.	5	4	3	2	1
8. I am comfortable depending on others and having them depend upon me.	5	4	3	2	1
9. It is important for me to feel independent and self-sufficient.	5	4	3	2	1
10. I often find that others are reluctant to get as close as I would like.	5	4	3	2	1
11. I sometimes worry that I will be hurt if I become too close to others.	5	4	3	2	1
12. I prefer not to depend on others or have them depend upon me.	5	4	3	2	1
13. I don't worry about being alone.	5	4	3	2	1
14. I find it difficult to depend upon others.	5	4	3	2	1
15. I sometimes worry that others don't value me as much as I value them.	5	4	3	2	1
16. I feel that others generally accept me.	5	4	3	2	1

Calculations for the GEP's Attachment Style Survey

(The highest result reflects your own assessment of your current attachment style)

___________ Secure (Add Q3+Q8+Q13+Q16)

___________ Avoidant (Add Q1+Q9+Q12+Q4)

___________ Anxious (Add Q2+Q10+Q7+Q15)

___________ Fearful (Add Q5+Q6+Q14+Q11)

Anxious Parents

Anxious parents can be very generous and attentive to their teen when their child is being a friend, openly valuing them, and being supportive and respectful. Remember, they want attention, and subconsciously, they try to get that through relationships. But as we know, relationships with teens can be fragile.

When they sense their teen is pulling away, anxious parents may trigger and act out—sometimes becoming overly clingy or critical.

They are not doing it on purpose. They are responding to their brain's distress, compounded by memories of previous relational disappointments. They might emotionally dysregulate when they perceive they have been disrespected, left out of the loop, betrayed, had secrets kept from them, or feel abandoned.

When this fear of abandonment is triggered (their greatest subconscious fear), they might panic or even have anxiety attacks.

If they demand that their child provide the support they want, it often pushes the child away.

The anxious parent will also tend to share their hurt feelings with their teen, not always in a healthy, loving way. Anxious parents are most likely externalizers and may blame their teen for the mess. "You made me feel this way."

Remember the teen's self-testimony in Tip #8? Here is the anxious parent self-testimony:

I want to be completely emotionally intimate with my teenager. Still, I often find they are reluctant to get as close as I would like. I am uncomfortable being without close relationships, but I sometimes worry that my teen doesn't value me as much as I value them.[1]

Where does this come from?

---

1. Adapted from Bartholomew and Horowitz, "Attachment Styles," 226–244.

Likely anxious parents have subconscious childhood memories stored in their *hippocampus* of being unhappy with the amount of attention they received from one or both of their parents. They may have felt truly loved by one and not the other, so it was an inconsistent experience. Their developing brain learned that they couldn't rely on love being there when they needed it.

This does not mean that their parents weren't good enough. It is simply their composite memory.

They are recognizable by a contradiction. They want support and friendship, but they often push people away when triggered (e.g., blaming, complaining, demanding, sharing their unhappiness, acting out, or raging).

What do teens say about their anxious parents?

- "My parents are often angry, abrasive, and critical. They overreact, carry grudges, and are demanding."
- "They tend not to be empathetic—it's all about them."
- "They are never satisfied—there is always something to criticize."
- "They never accept responsibility for the mess."
- "Bottom line, they are high maintenance. All my friends can see it too."

In answer to the Question #1: "Am I worthy of your love?" The subconscious answer in an anxious parent's brain is, "No, most of the time I don't feel confident in that. I need constant demonstrations of how much my teen loves me—I need it."

Question #2: "Can I count on my teen?" Answer: "I hope so. I need it—and if I sense I can't, I will trigger."

It is obvious why there is so much friction between anxious

parents and anxious children. Both are externalizers. Both will trigger quickly and blame the other.

Anxious parents struggle with avoidant children as well. Avoidant children often want space, which the anxious parent might interpret as abandonment. Anxious parents may respond by pushing the child for more intimacy and attention, which can lead to resentment and a nasty, recurring cycle.

Author Chen says it all too well, "Being in a relationship with someone who is acting out an anxious attachment style can feel like dealing with an angry customer while staffing a support/complaint desk."[2]

Avoidant Parents

Avoidant parents get stressed when they feel others are becoming too close.

Remember the teen's self-testimony from Tip #8? Here is the avoidant parent testimony:

I am comfortable without a close emotional relationship with my teenager. It is very important to me to feel independent and self-sufficient, and I prefer not to depend on others or to have others depend on me.[3]

These parents can come across as self-reliant.

They can be passive-aggressive when things go wrong, meaning they typically do not openly criticize but express their displeasure indirectly.

They tend to talk about ideas rather than themselves or their

---

2. Annie Chen, *The Attachment Theory Workbook: Powerful Tools to Promote Understanding, Increase Stability, and Build Lasting Relationships* (Berkeley, CA: Althea Press, 2019), 39.
3. Adapted from Bartholomew and Horowitz, "Attachment Styles," 226–244.

feelings and prefer to dispose of conflict quickly—they are peace-keepers rather than peacemakers.

Per Chen again:

Avoidance behaviors can show up in a variety of ways, like outright ignoring conflict, denying what happened, or escaping discomfort through substances. But it can also be subtler, such as people pleasing or focusing so much on being helpful to others that you neglect yourself. It can be any response that protects you from feeling shame or inadequate."[4]

Avoidant parents don't talk much about themselves. They don't chase the spotlight—or make their own needs known, and they get weary of others who do.

One of their key complaints in relationships is that others need too much from them. If others are too needy, they can feel stressed or inadequate and shift into avoidance mode.

Their focus is on logic and reason, not feelings.

How did this come about? During childhood, avoidant adults didn't feel supported, celebrated, or validated by core caregivers. Chen is helpful here:

"Their fondest memories involved being by themselves for hours in the woods, daydreaming or inventing entire plays with stuffed animals in their rooms."[5]

Perhaps parental support and affection came when the child did something right, or was *right*, i.e., recognized for intelligence, beauty, athleticism, personality, or talents.

---

4. Ibid, 50.
5. Ibid. 51.

What do teens say about their avoidant parents?

- "My parents don't want to deal with problems, are uncomfortable with conflict and struggle to resolve them."
- "They want to keep things at a rational level and avoid messy emotions."
- "Explanations can be very one-sided: 'Because I am your parent.'"
- "They are difficult to attune to."
- "I would say they are passive-aggressive. Quickly withdrawing when triggered."

In answer to Question #1: "Am I worthy of your love?" Their answer is, "Maybe, but I don't allow myself to be in that place where I need my teen's love. Too much stress and work."

Question #2: "Can I count on my teen?" I keep these expectations low. I am good on my own.

Fearful Parents

Fearful parents are a combination of both.

They can be both needy and avoidant at the same time, or cycle between the two.

This person often vacillates between longing and fear, demanding connection and then distancing, and even attacking when connection is offered.

This type of response is called disorganized attachment in children.

It is termed fearful avoidant attachment in adults and is associated with especially high distress in adult relationships.[6]

They would agree with the following:

I am somewhat uncomfortable getting close to my teen. I want emotionally close relationships, but I find it difficult to trust my teen completely or to depend on them. I sometimes worry that I will be hurt if I allow myself to become too close to my teenager.[7]

It is typically seen in those with some history of trauma, abuse, or neglect. These parents may intensely seek their teen's attention and then intensely try to avoid their child out of fear, vacillating between highly anxious and highly avoidant strategies.

They may blow up or shut down emotionally.

To the core questions:

"Am I worthy of your love?" They might answer, "I do not think so."

"Can I count on you?" "I want to, but no, it is too risky."

So, parent, what can you do?

If you want to lean into being more secure, there is something you can do.

The creator of your brain dwells in your inner being. The Spirit is very powerful and is passionate about making you feel the love of God that Jesus purchased for you 2000 years ago.

Spiritual growth is less about using your attachment-style tendencies and working harder to fix your relationship with God and others.

---

6. Johnson, Susan M. *Hold Me Tight: Seven Conversations for a Lifetime of Love.* New York: Little, Brown and Company, 2008.

7. Adapted from Bartholomew and Horowitz, "Attachment Styles," 226–244.

Rather, it is more about you depending on His power. How?

1. Ask. Repeat the *SUG* at least twice a day. Access by faith, through the Spirit in your inner being, the height, width, length, and depth of the love of Christ for you— as you are—in whatever quadrant you are. And the same for your child, in whatever quadrant they are. God loves people the same in each quadrant.
2. See *The Dance (www.the-dance.online)* and complete the exercise.
3. Ephesians 3. Ask the Spirit to fill you to the fullness of God. This will not happen fully until heaven, but even experiencing some of that fullness now will be noticeable. Think of it as your empty cup filling up with a little more enoughness and connectedness that only God can birth in us. Imagine if you felt how enough you are to God and how that would make you less needy for enoughness from others. It would be a miracle. You would be less anxious and more secure.

And what if you began to feel what a perfect, permanent, life-giving, trusted relationship was like?

This relationship is yours, not because of what you do, but because of what Jesus did—less guilt, less shame. You don't fear disconnection as much, and you evolve toward a secure attachment. You can draw closer to your teen—because you have a new heart with a different motivation and less fear.

One last thing. Please listen to this worship song by Maverick City and performed by Elevation Worship, "Jireh." Here is the QR code. This is the message that all insecure GEPs need—and we are all insecure parents to one degree or another.

Review

When your teen finally opens up about the bullying, the breakup, the scary thoughts—your midbrain wants to leap in with solutions, lectures, or "It's not that bad."

Resist. Be aware that you are being driven by your own attachment style—not your child's needs.

The most powerful adolescent attunement is emotional presence:

- Eye contact that says, "I'm with you."
- Mirroring the feeling "That sounds crushing."
- Silence that feels safe, not awkward.
- A hug or a hand on the shoulder (if they'll let you).

You're teaching their nervous system: "Big feelings don't have to be faced alone."

Only after they feel fully heard do you ask, "Want my thoughts, or just need me to listen?"

Most of the time, they pick listening. And their brain logs another point toward secure attachment.

Tip #11
Good Enough Parents Understand Adolescent Attunement Better than Non-Good-Enough Parents

*(A sense of enoughness is built on one specific,
delighted affirmation at a time)*

Welcome to Tip #11. This is a dynamite tip. If you miss all the rest and do this one thing, you will notice a difference, maybe not immediately. Still, it is a serious investment in your child's future self and your future relationship with them.

I said at the beginning that this is not meant to be a how-to manual—more of a why.

Parent-teen communication can be a challenging quagmire. Parents think they are being perfectly clear with their child, but the child doesn't listen—and vice versa. I have found that it is often not about *being clear*.

Here are some real-world examples of miscommunication and language translation errors that highlight how words alone can fall short in parent-teen conversations.

- The name Coca-Cola in China was first rendered as Ke-kou-ke-la. Sounds good, but unfortunately, it can be translated as "Bite the wax tadpole."
- Also in Chinese, the Kentucky Fried Chicken slogan: "Finger-lickin' good" came out as: "Eat your fingers off."
- When Parker Pen marketed a ballpoint pen in Mexico, its advertisements were supposed to say: "It won't leak in your pocket and embarrass you." But what they ended up with in Spanish was: "It won't leak in your pocket and make you pregnant."

While language and words are important, the larger context of communication is even more so. Good communication with your teen must be dripping with *attunement*—to coin a phrase, dripping with *adolescent attunement*.

Here is a definition of attunement by author Christina Reese:[1]

Attunement is being connected to a person in such a way that you respond to the needs of the other person before that need is even expressed. Attunement is the building block of trust. When a need is met before it is even voiced, it builds confidence in the person who met the need. In turn, trust is built.

This attunement can be with an infant or an adolescent, and of course, this is what God does in spiritual attunement.

It is how our brains were created.

------

1. Reese, Christina. *Attachment: 60 Trauma-Informed Assessment and Treatment Interventions Across the Lifespan.* Eau Claire, WI: PESI Publishing, 2018. See more discussion on attunement in Tip #5.

They respond to repeated, creative expressions of love and attunement.

Adolescent attunement begins to build or rebuild a trust bond that can insulate your teen from many negative influences. It promotes the trust necessary for them to seek advice, accept guidance, and curb some of the emotional dysregulation and acting out that inevitably creeps into adolescence.

Remember what's going on in your child's brain?

It's often a zoo in there—a veritable blender. If you think your child is not listening, not paying attention, or prioritizing other things over you, you are not entirely wrong.

And it is not all their fault.

In the dark shadows of their emotionally and chemically altered mid-brains, even while they are looking straight at you and listening, their brain is busy wondering where they can get a shot of more enoughness and connectedness.

The subconscious fallback answer as they look into your eyes is, "Anywhere but here!"

Remember the two constant subconscious questions your teen is asking? "Can I count on you?" and "Am I worthy of your love?"

What do they see in your face and in your eyes when you are talking to them? What is their unconscious emotional brain's answer based on your reaction to them?

Think back to the *Still Face Experiment* (Tip #6) and infant attunement. From the one-year-old's perspective, what was happening? The attunement was communicated in two ways: the means (face, voice, tone, inflections, singular attention, eye dilation and expression) and the message (words). Infant attunement is powerful, igniting healing chemicals in both parties, especially the important bonding chemicals.

When the child saw her mom's non-still-faced, adoring gaze, the foundational communication received by her midbrain (message and means) was that she was special to her mom and that there was nowhere else on the planet her mom would rather be than right in front of her daughter.

She was subconsciously experiencing enoughness and connectedness long before she was aware of what those meant. Cortisol levels drop (fear cycle), and dopamine and oxytocin rise (feel good and bonding).

It's the same with adolescent attunement.

GEPs do adolescent attunement more than NGEPs.

Good Messaging Is More Than Language

Below is a template for you. Read this letter from God, your heavenly parent, to you. In this case, you are acting as the adolescent—a stand-in relative to God.

I use this letter in *The Dance* and *The Forgiving Path (Tip #14)*. Many people say this was one of the pinnacles in their online experiences.

You will see why.

Imagine seeing the face of Jesus as you read (*the means*). You can tell He is so happy to be with you.

He is not Still-Faced toward you.

His eyebrows are raised; his pupils are dilated.

There is no other place in the universe He would rather be.

Can you imagine it?

Now hear the words.

My Beloved,

Do you know how much I adore you? When I look deep in your eyes—into your weary and beat-up soul, do you know what I feel? I am stunned at what I see. I made you for a particular purpose of great glory and creativity. I specifically chose your eye color, your hair color, and your stubbornness because no other colors or traits would do.

You have been resistant to My love. I know your struggle better than even you do. You have had your reasons for it, but now it is time for you to be loved with the love that, up until now, you could only dream of from a distance. This is what your soul has longed for since you were a child. This is the love you have been searching for all your life in all the wrong places. I love you as you are— right now—with all the warts and wrinkles, all the scars and mistakes you've made. I look at you and know who you really are. I love you far more than you could love yourself. You look in the mirror, and you see distortion and fractures —scars. I only see your deep, residing beauty unscarred. Look at your reflection in my eyes—then you will see and know.

You don't need to dress up for me. I am not a fan of masks. You have many fears. No doubt, you may imagine that I, too, will not love you, that I would be ashamed of what I see, or that I would be angry at you, as others have been. But that will not happen. I only desire to honor you with great love and glory.

I invite you to come into my embrace just to be held and adored—as you are. You can do nothing to earn my love. It cannot be earned. I paid for it 2000 years ago. Now it is perfectly yours forever. Know this: My love will not leave you as you are. My love heals.

Come to Me as I am. Do not delay. Come. If anyone thirsts, let them come to me. I will quench their thirst, and I know your soul is very thirsty. Come and drink freely. Do not hesitate. Do not be ashamed. Come. It is time to leave the darkness and shadows that plague you. Come, enter the light.

I love you,
Jesus

This is a great example of *spiritual attunement*. One child psychologist said, "Every child needs at least one adult who is irrationally crazy about him or her."[2]

How does it feel that God is irrationally crazy about you?

Are feel-good chemicals lighting up your brain?

Are you feeling more enough and more connected to Him because of this spiritual attunement?

More *secure*?

This is exactly what your teen is craving for—from God and from you.

I have also written such a letter for your teen—in my voice— not yours. Consider it a template for you to use.

For now, sit back and breathe, be aware of the emotions you're feeling as you read.

My son/daughter,

Do you know how much I adore you? When I look deep in your eyes—into your weary and beat-up soul, do you know what I feel? I am stunned at what I see. You were made for a particular purpose of great glory and creativity. I am sure of it. It all fits: your eye color, your hair color, and your stubbornness, because no other colors or traits would do. I can't wait to see how you will change the world. I will always be your biggest fan. I will always have your back— no matter what.

I know you have your struggles. You want to know that you are good enough. This is what your soul has longed for since you were a child. To be clear, I love you as you are— right now—with all the warts and wrinkles—all your mistakes. You look in the mirror, and you see distortion and

---

2. Urie Bronfenbrenner, *Making Human Beings Human: Bioecological Perspectives on Human Development* (Thousand Oaks, CA: Sage Publications, 2005), **page 262**.

fractures—scars. I only see your deep, residing beauty—unscarred. Look at your reflection in my eyes—then you will see and know.

You don't need to dress up for me—or lose weight, or put on weight, or be smarter. I am not a fan of masks, of faking it.

You have fears; it is perfectly normal. Maybe you imagine that you will disappoint me, or that I will stop loving you or stop liking you, that I will be ashamed of what I see, that I will go still-faced when you most need me. But that will not happen.

Come to me—as you are. You can do nothing to earn my love, or to earn any more of it. It is already yours.

Love, Mom/Dad

Attunement is not just the words. It is the message, sure, but also the heart. Don't just put it in an envelope on their bureau for them to read. The *Still Face* mother didn't just call it in. She was there in all her glory—message and means.

Here's a thought. Get your teen's attention. Take them to a special dinner or hike. Social media devices off. Read this aloud to them face-to-face. Your face, your eyes looking into theirs—and show them how valuable they are to you. They are enough for you and worthy of your connection.

They should see it—and feel it. They should be able to tell that you are excited to be with them, and there is nowhere else in the world that you would rather be than in front of them right now.

It may be awkward the first time—and the second time—for both of you.

I get that.

They may love it but not be willing to show it. Maybe it won't change anything in the short term.

But here is what we know about the human brain. In the *Still*

Face Experiment, when the mother's still-face ended, there was a powerful change in the infant's brain—lots of chemicals involved.

She couldn't stop it.

Neither can your teenager.

Does it fix your child?

Are you kidding? Of course not!

Remember, GEPs see adolescence as an enoughness and connectedness redo season. It will likely take the entire decade—an ongoing battle for their sense of enoughness and connectedness.

Our long-term strategy isn't to fix, but to creatively and repeatedly express our love—or better, Jesus' love for the unlovable, unloved, and unlovely—through you to them—as they are.

This letter idea is only a one-shot thing, a shot across the bow. This expression of adolescent attunement should be ongoing—drip, drip, drip. Be creative.

Parenting Your Young Child

My son-in-law, Rev. Jeff Buster, speaks about the importance of ongoing attunement *movements* by parents of younger children and of *random* acts of affection over a significant period.

You can listen to my three interviews with Jeff in the podcast series "Gospel Parenting," first aired in June 2021, from my Gospel Rant Podcast.

Here are some ideas. Randomly during the week, surprise your child or teen by saying:

- "George, do you know how much I love you?"
- "Betty, do you know I am a big fan of yours?"
- "If I could, I would buy stock in you."

- "I believe that you can change the world. How can I support you?"
- "Why is it that I like you so much?"

You get the idea—scatter random and unexpected comments throughout the day and week.

But you ask, "Dr. Bill, there has been a lot of water under the bridge. My child would not believe it when I tell them that I love them or like them."

"We don't do that in my family—not anymore."

"We no longer trust each other—there are lots of unresolved issues."

"Honestly, I am not sure I could say that I like them—there has been a lot of wounding on both sides. So now what?"

You are not alone. This is only the first step. It will likely be awkward or worse. You can do it.

Attunement must be repeated over and over again.

Let me give you some straight-up theology. The Holy Spirit adores your Christian teen and loves them as much as He loves the Father and the Son. You think you have a beef against your teen—think about God's.

But 2000 years ago, strictly because of what Jesus did for them, God loved them to death.

They cannot mess it up.

They cannot fall short.

They cannot push God away.

**God doesn't know how not to love them
or how to abandon them.**

Though God is likely disappointed by all your child's (and your) actions and choices to one degree or another, God is no longer offended or disappointed in *them*.

All the "less than perfect" choices and actions were carried on Jesus' shoulders at the Cross. It is finished.

If that is the case, and you're struggling to love your child, then your bigger problem is that you are—to one degree or another—out of sync with the Holy Spirit in you. Humanly speaking, you can justify your position, but clearly, you are out of step with God.

Not a good place to be—am I right?

It is not all your fault.

Your brain is likely flashing red lights when I talk about vulnerability and lacking dignity, protecting your heart, and pursuing your teen again. Your brain is designed to protect you from hurt—and particularly, relational hurt—the worst kind. Your brain might fiercely resist this approach. I get it.

Let's try something different. Here's what you *can* do, and what your brain will let you do.

Ask the Spirit to *make* you feel God's love for your teen.

I am talking about a miracle—on the level of the parting of the Red Sea.

"God, right now, I don't love or even like my teen. If it is going to happen, you must *make* me feel enough of Your love for them so that it is noticeable, even by my child—not perfectly, but noticeably."

Then, when you begin to feel that love and like a little, and feel a little more motivated to risk being hurt again—the miracle of a new heart that is more for reconciliation than protection, another God-thing—go with it.

For the next 30 days, pray that prayer. Say the *SUG* aloud repeatedly to yourself, at least twice a day.

Go through the *Forgiving Path* (See Tip #14) with some of the specific hurts from your teen in mind.

After 30 days, do a self-check. Any difference? I am sure you will notice something positive. It's a long-term strategy, not an easy fix, for you or for them.

GEPs know the importance of regular spiritual attunement for themselves and adolescent attunement for their child.

In the case of badly busted relationships, this could take a while and will require more than just your hard work to accomplish anything of lasting value.

"Almost dead" relationships require a miracle.

But God does his best work with almost dead things.

Good news, the Spirit's passion in you and in your Christian teen is to make each of you feel the height, width, length, and depth of the love of Christ for you and for the other, beginning right now (Eph. 3:14-21).

You can do it. I would love to hear about your experience. Bill@gospel-app.com.

Review

Your teen's brain is drowning in comparison and criticism (social media + inner critic + Satan).

Your voice is still the most powerful, human counterweight.

Catch them being:

- Kind when no one was watching.
- Honest when lying would've been easier.
- Brave when they were terrified.
- Funny, creative, generous, thoughtful.

Then go over the top:

- "I just watched you help your sister without being asked.
  Are you kidding me? I'm the luckiest parent alive."
- "I heard how you stood up to that friend pressuring you
  —my respect for you just doubled."

Specific, delighted, slightly embarrassing celebration rewires the "I'm not enough" lie faster than any lecture ever could.

Do it three times a week and watch the secure attachment grow.

Tip #12

Good Enough Parents Know How to Deal with Teen Conflict More than Non-Good-Enough Parents

(Remember it's not all their fault—or yours.)

GEPs understand that:

1. Their teenager's behavior is not entirely reasonable. Their teen's prefrontal cortex (PFC) is not fully online, and it is not *all* their fault.
2. God loves your Christian child as they are—insecure or secure—He loves teens in all quadrants the same, no more and no less.
3. Adolescence is a time for an attachment style redo—second only to infancy—where God, you, and your child can reshape some of their inner wiring.
4. The passion of the Holy Spirit is to make your teen experience more enoughness and connectedness from God—beginning now. That should make a noticeable difference in their social and emotional capabilities.

5. Every opportunity should be taken to lavish your teen
   with adolescent attunement—at least 30% of the time. It
   won't fix things, that's for Heaven, but it should be
   noticeable. The hope is that they become your BFF by
   the time they are 30.

This twelfth tip is so important.

Suppose things are going well with you and your teen. People are talking—more than passing grunts like "Fine" or "Whatever." There is some interest at the dinner table. Relatively speaking, no major conflicts—and then BOOM—all hell breaks loose.

Your teen has a request: "Mom, can I talk to you about something? I want…. Can I …?" "All the other kids are doing it. Everyone's going."

So, for example, your 15-year-old "Harry" wants to go to a friend's house for a sleepover, but the friend's parents won't be there. You may disagree, but ten times out of ten, this is a sketchy idea.

It is not reasonable.

There are so many red flags, possible long-term consequences, and unsafe conditions.

GEPs aren't drawn into attempting a reasonable dialogue. It won't work. Your teen is not reasonable at this point.

We've all been there. There is rarely a "Mr. Miyagi Karate Kid" moment when words of wisdom totally convince the teen to act against their mid-brain's unreasonable, risky want-to.

These moments are almost always mine fields.

The older your teen is, the less "Because I told you so" does anything but make the situation worse.

If this were a business, there would be several helpful strategic models. Skilled, rational negotiators who work for hours to find the ZOPA—the zone of possible agreement. Then there is the BATNA—the Best Alternative to a Negotiated Agreement.

Working toward a common end, business negotiators:

1. Identify the problem
2. Collect information
3. Assess the alternatives
4. Weigh the evidence
5. Select among alternatives
6. Take action
7. Review the decision and the consequences

GEPs understand that the above strategy is a pipe dream with teens. Dealing with teens is not reasonable; dealing with teens who are craving for enoughness and connectedness (Quadrants #2-4) is certainly not reasonable.

Reason seldom works, particularly if there are trust breakdowns.

GEPs recognize that their teen's PFC is still under construction, making reasoning ineffective.

The PFC protects against impulsive or risky decisions and helps them be aware of the long-term consequences of their choices. It is not working at full capacity. Their brain's car is running, but no one's driving—there's no steering wheel or brakes.

So, a Non-GEP's strategy of trying to reason with their teen is unlikely to work. Stop it!

These "negotiations" often reverse any movement toward Quadrant #1 and further entrench your teen into one of the three insecure quadrants.

Unfortunately, the word "no" can be a massive trigger for such teens. It can feel like a rejection, disapproval, or that the parent is just mean and untrustworthy.

GEPs grasp that in this moment, your child's brain isn't about right or wrong, wise or unwise. It has a higher priority. The situation is about your teen's deep, subconscious need for more enoughness and connectedness.

This conflict is your open door to express your love for them—adolescent attunement.

Consider the person with an addiction. It's similar in some sense. All the teen's mid-brain can think about and talk about is being in a room with friends who often make them feel a little more enoughness and connectedness than they feel now—just what the doctor ordered. You don't want to be in the way of that movement. Their mid-brain is longing for this. Let's drill down further.

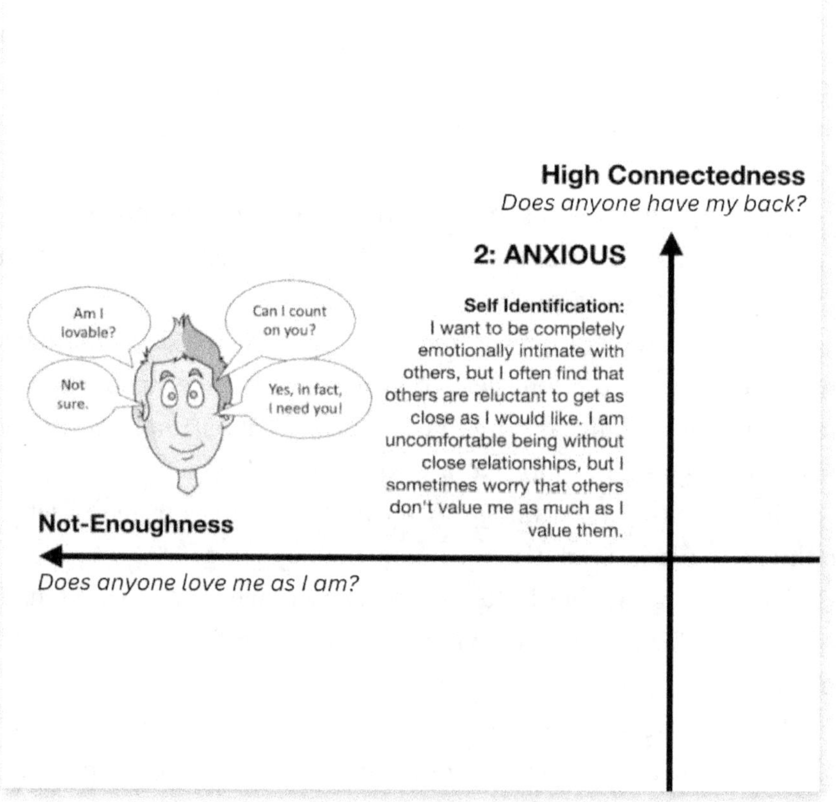

If your child tends toward Quadrant #2—anxiousness—they look for an experience of enoughness in the measuring gaze of their peers—right or wrong—it is what it is. Think of an empty enoughness cup that desperately needs to be filled—now.

The sleepover could bring some coveted enoughness-filling.

Red flags? What red flags?

Not going would, at best, do nothing, at worst, lower their assessment in the measuring gaze of their friends.

FOMO, right?[1]

The sleepover isn't about reason or being right, careful or wise. Your child is never going to verbalize, "My worth cup is leaky, and I need filling. Why are you against me feeling more enough and connected?"

For most NGEPs, laying down the law, offering reasons, and engaging in dialogue are the go-to approaches.

They may try to reason with their child, misunderstanding that their child's brain is simply not being reasonable, especially now. The moment they start to negotiate, their child's defense mechanism soars. "Because I said so…" is the worst. But I've done it.

GEPs realize that more important than making the *right* (whatever that means) strategic, ideal decision here is to take this golden opportunity—when your child's enoughness and connectedness needs are flaring—to communicate to your teen that you are their biggest fan.

Remember the random and undignified acts of love from the last tip? Here is a huge opportunity for both.

This is an opportunity targeted to make your teen feel adored, respected, and honored by you and to convince them that you would never shame them—particularly in front of their peers—nor make them feel like a little child, stupid, or incapable of making good decisions on their own.

"Honey, I adore you. I am your biggest fan. I will always have your back. If something happens, you know that I am here for you. Always. You are special, and I can't wait to see how you will change the world."

---

1. Fear of Missing Out

Look into their eyes and let them see for themselves that you adore them as they are, not based upon this issue, right or wrong.

Done regularly, these are the things that will begin to nudge their mid-brain away from the insecure quadrants toward Quadrant #1, secure.

It will pay off when these "dialogues" pop up. It should be noticeable as your teen's internal working model begins to be rewired somewhat.

Does it work? So, let's say, after some concentrated adolescent attunement time, you say something parent-like, such as, "Harry, if parents are not there, you are not going."

Will they take it calmly since you've attuned some?

Absolutely not.

I mentioned that they are somewhat like unreasonable addicts longing for enoughness and connectedness. No, this won't go down without some emotional dysregulation. GEPs expect some of this.

GEPs aren't thinking that they do this a couple of times and, abracadabra, their child will be okay with whatever the decision is or will see the logic. What? Are you kidding me?

Of course not.

GEPs know they are leaning into long-term incremental movement from insecurity to security. Their love—accessed through the Holy Spirit in their inner being—is patient and loves the unlovable, even the dysregulated, the insecure.

That's all there is.

They have an entire decade to push back, and they will likely need every moment of it.

Think baby-steps toward the security of Quadrant #1.

If, due to their current attachment style, they blow-up at a 6— big blow-up, slamming doors, threatening to run away, and the rest —GEPs do the incremental adolescent attunement so that next time the blow-up is a 5.5. If their cup of enoughness and connectedness is filled a little more because of what you do, you might even get it down to a 5.2.

Count that as a win.

GEPs are investing for the long term. Your teen may never understand and may even hold a grudge—but there is a greater chance they will become one of your best friends once that PFC kicks in.

Review

Consequences are necessary. Boundaries are loving. But never let a consequence sever the emotional connection.

Classic mistake: Teen breaks curfew → parent explodes → three-day silent treatment → teen feels abandoned → acts out worse.

Good Enough version: Teen breaks curfew → The message: "You messed up. I still adore you. We're on the same team."

Secure teens can handle firm boundaries because they're rooted in unbreakable love.

Insecure teens test boundaries endlessly because they're trying to answer, "If I push hard enough, will you leave?"

Your calm, connected, consistent answer: "Never."

That's how you parent a teen towards Quadrant #1: Secure—one repaired rupture, one delighted celebration, one emotionally present conversation at a time.

And you only need to get it right 30% of the time.

You've got this.

Now, ask for power today—Ephesians 3 style.

Tip #13
Good Enough Parents Apologize More than Non-Good-Enough Parents

(Worldly sorrow kills relationships. Godly sorrow resurrects them.)

Welcome to this extremely practical Tip #13.

Many of us were raised to think that parents should never say they were sorry. Can anyone tell me why? In fact, the opposite is true.

By far, the best father moments with my kids, the ones that made the biggest difference in our relationship even today, were when I apologized for something. Believe me, there were many opportunities.

My adult children now tease me for some of the parenting I subjected them to. It is a miracle that we can laugh about it. You can get there too.

Here are two things that occur when you don't say you're sorry.

First, It Sabotages the Relationship

Our brain's hippocampus stores both implicit and explicit memories, along with the emotions associated with them.

If you did something and your teen was embittered, felt betrayed, or you broke your word, that memory and the emotions stay stored away until heaven, or until healing takes place. Over the years, unresolved conflict can turn into entrenched, hidden resentment, bitterness, avoidance, and even hatred.

It communicates disrespect, which is far worse than Still Face.

In attachment-style language, not regularly apologizing to your teen empties their cups of enoughness and connectedness.

That nasty inner critical voice is likely to take the opportunity to say something like, "I guess my parents don't think I am good enough for them to apologize for what they did."

GEPs will say sorry more than Non-GEPs.

Second, It Misses a Teachable Moment

Imagine. You fell short. You broke your word. You said something you now regret. Sitting your teenager down, you say, "Son, daughter, I am so sorry. I told you that I love you as you are. But in that moment, I didn't. Please forgive me."

Acknowledging our mistakes towards our teens is the most powerful form of adolescent attunement that I know of.

GEPs do not miss this opportunity.

Let me share an example of a time when I got it right—they were way too few and far between.

It was with my two oldest children when they were young. We had finally put them to bed—a nightly struggle, it seemed. Looking back, I can see that it made me angry, partly because it made me feel like a failure as a father, out of control, disrespected, and not good enough.

That's on me, but it's quite a common feeling for parents.

Well, this evening, my wife and I were "discussing" something. Harsh things were being said and loudly. Then there was a quiet tap, tap on the bedroom door.

I knew who it was. Our disobedient children. It made me angry. I stormed over to the door, flung it open, and barked at them for being out of bed and not obeying.

I must have said it loudly, because they didn't say a thing; instead, they quickly turned and ran off to their rooms.

Me? I thought, at last, I did this right. Now my kids will respect me. I just need to turn up the testosterone the next time I put them to bed.

A couple of days later—that's right, that is on me too— I was driving them to school. They were in the back seat. I finally noticed that they were quiet.

My kids were never quiet when they were together, and they certainly weren't looking at me in the rearview mirror.

I believe the Holy Spirit grabbed me. Out of the blue, I understood how I had hurt them. Not only had I done something unjust and wrong, but I had put a tear in our relationship.

I was crushed.

I pulled over on the street, opened the back door, and started crying.

The Spirit moved me to ask a single question. "So, can you tell me how it made you feel when I yelled at you the other night?" They told me. They had immediate answers.

Whew, that was hard to hear.

"I am so sorry that I did that to you. I never want to make you feel unloved or think that I don't adore you. That was not about you. That was about daddy. Will you forgive me?"

We hugged.

There was powerful relational healing, a God-sized miracle.

God turned my disrespect of them into them feeling respected—at the heart level.

We can laugh about it now, but it could have gone badly just as easily. It was one of the greatest post-infant attuning moments for my children.

Okay, you may expect me to tell you to apologize more often. I am not going to do that.

We do what we want to do.

The problem is our internal motivation. You are not sorry; otherwise, you would say so, right? Therefore, I am not going to shame you into faking it or trying harder. I am going to point you to the source of true redemptive healing: genuine sorrow.

"Sorry" Counterfeits

Before I explore *genuine* apologies, here are some of the common counterfeits that parents can and probably are doing on their own:

- Excuses ("I misunderstood what you meant.")
- Self-justifications ("I meant well, it just came out wrong.")
- Blaming others ("Look, my supervisor beat me up earlier and I was upset, okay?")
- Blaming the context ("Well, I wouldn't have done it except that I was having a bad day, and you just happened along. I've been under stress lately; it's not about you; it's about my miserable life.")
- Blaming the victim ("You should have said something.")
- Portraying yourself as the *real* victim.
- Ignoring the violation ("Time heals all wounds.")
- Blaming history ("My father treated me the very same way. I guess I get it from him.")

- Minimizing the violation ("Well, I didn't mean to hurt you. That wasn't my intent. Look, it wasn't all that bad, was it?")
- Not accepting responsibility ("I am sorry if you felt hurt.")
- Giving a quick apology to get it over with ("Look, I am sorry, I really am. Let's move on from here, okay?")
- Demanding forgiveness ("I said I was sorry; the Christian thing would be for you to forgive me.")
- Issuing quick promises to reform ("I messed up, but I promise, I'll never do it again.")
- Whitewashing the account to make yourself look good.

These responses are normal. Still, GEPs need more. So how do GEPs become *more sorry*?

The Saying-Sorry Passage

Check out 2 Corinthians 7: 10-11 (the "saying sorry" passage). Paul says that there are two types of "sorry."

One is of the world.

One is of God.

One leads to the death of relationships.

The other leads to the resurrection of wounded or dead relationships. Enough said.

Godly sorrow brings repentance that leads to salvation and leaves no regret, but worldly sorrow brings death. See what this godly sorrow has produced in you: what earnestness, what eagerness to clear yourselves, what indignation, what alarm, what longing, what concern, what readiness to see justice done. At every point you have proved yourselves to be innocent in this matter. *(2 Cor 7:10-11)*

Godly sorrow is special. It isn't passive at all. It *makes* us do and feel something. Paul lists eight things that Godly sorrow *produced* in and among the Corinthians—things it *made* them feel and do. This is not just a theoretical, philosophical dogma to Paul. Godly sorrow was an actual creative power that manifested itself observably within the brain of the Corinthians.

Godly sorrow produced:

- a fresh experience of their relationship with God.
- an earnestness (maybe a seriousness to deal with all the relational issues).
- a new motivation.
- indignation (maybe at how they caused relational breakdown).
- fear (maybe fear of God, referring to a healthy relationship with God).
- relational longing (maybe longing to be reconciled).
- relational zeal (a new motivation likely to be reconciled with the one they hurt).
- a readiness to see justice done (relational breaches often require vindication and justice).

Did you hear the word *relational* repeatedly? I could have said *attachment*.

The Corinthians had serious enoughness and connectedness issues. Then God broke in and made them feel this "I'm sorry" that only comes from God—that brings life to dead relationships.

I don't know if they did it with their teenagers. I'd like to think that they did.

GEPs know that though "I'm sorry!" comes from God, our part is to ask for it regularly. Being "sorry" with genuine "sorry" can ignite new life into our old, tattered relationships.

It causes a rewiring of attachment styles toward Quadrant #1.

Worldly "I am sorry" isn't all bad. It is just very tepid and weak in comparison. Paul says it murders.

What is the key difference between Godly and worldly "I am sorry?"

One is a superhuman miracle that comes exclusively from God. The other does not need God.

Here is a prayer I wrote to help GEPs ask for godly sorrow. Sit back and soak it in.

God, I am beginning to see that I blew it again. What is wrong with me that I would act so destructively or casually toward this person—or any person, for that matter? Even more tragic is that I have been fighting for so long to avoid admitting my guilt. I have been trying every trick in the book. It has not worked. I see that now. Holy Spirit, I plead with You, make me feel Your love for the person that I hurt. Give me Your Godly sorrow deep in my inner being, until I begin to feel new life, a new love for the person that I disrespected, and a new desire to do the hard work to heal the community that I shattered. Remind me of how much You love me, adore me, and am proud of me, all strictly because of Christ's efforts on my behalf. I will need that assurance of Your undying love for me as I plunge into these dangerous waters of repentance. Amen.

You can begin to see, along with other recent tips, how asking God for His power repeatedly is a powerful remedy against your midbrain, which is full of insecurities. This is the time to be empowered to shift toward Quadrant #1.

Godly sorrow and your words, a powerful combination.

Review

There are two kinds of "I'm sorry" (2 Corinthians 7:10–11):

Worldly sorrow = excuses, minimizing, blaming, and quick fixes. It feels better for five minutes and slowly murders relationships.

Godly sorrow = earnestness, indignation at the hurt caused, alarm, longing, zeal, readiness to make things right. It feels terrible at first, but it brings dead relationships back to life.

Godly sorrow isn't something you manufacture. It's a miracle you ask for.

GEPs ask for godly sorrow regularly. It's a sure way to move a teen's internal working model toward secure attachment.

Tip #14

Good Enough Parents Forgive More than Non-Good-Enough Parents

(You can't forgive. Doesn't that explain so much?)

When I talk to parents about forgiveness, I get an earful of opinions, particularly about older teens:

"I can't keep forgiving his behavior."

"I've forgiven her a lot; I don't know how to forgive anymore."

"I believe in forgiveness, but when does it stop being *forgiveness* and start being *taken advantage of*?"

"Isn't that enabling?"

And the classic, "But you have no idea what my child has done to me."

Our kids have the same feelings about forgiving their parents as their parents have about forgiving their kids.

Here is an extended quote from a blog on the "Parent Cue" website by Tim Walker. He had me— until the end. But it is worth reading.

"I'm sorry." When those words are delivered by the high-pitched voice of a child, they melt you. Of course I'll forgive you, you think. How could I not?

Even if there is a huge mess behind her.

Bookcases are knocked over.

The dog is barking.

The cat is perched on top of the chandelier.

A team of people are unrolling "condemned tape" across your house.

But when you hear "I'm sorry" and see those big brown eyes, the anger and frustration lessen a little bit. Sure, they may be staring at a corner for a while or be contained in their room, but you'll forgive them. There's a reason God makes them so cute at that age.

But as they grow older, "sorry" gets a little more difficult to digest.

Like when your middle schooler looks you in the face and lies.

Or when she says she's going one place, and ends up at another.

Or you stumble across a social media account and find your child has been bashing you.

Or your high schooler wrecks the car.

Or in a teenage hormonal rage, he or she took a verbal shot at your most vulnerable point.

There are times when your child's actions will feel more personal.

There are moments when their words will cut you deeply.

And you'll find yourself in a unique position.

You may not want to forgive them.

*In fact, it will feel as painful, if not more, as the betrayal of a
    close friend.*

You'll be sad.

You'll be mad.

You'll feel like a failure.

You'll feel like they've failed you.

You'll wonder if you can ever trust them again.

*You may find yourself scrambling, wondering where do we
    go from here?*

Forgiveness won't come so easily.

Those big brown eyes won't make it all go away.

Your child should have known better.

He or she should have made different choices.

*The pangs of guilt, preying on your own parental insecuri-
    ties, will whisper in the back of your head.*

I wish I could offer an easy answer here.

*But when you are that hurt, one thing becomes painfully
    clear, forgiving is a choice.*

And so you have to choose to forgive.

It doesn't mean there aren't consequences for their actions.

Or that trust isn't damaged.

But you choose to forgive.

Because if you don't, it will destroy you.

And it will destroy your relationship with your child.

You choose to forgive the hurt.

You choose to forgive the disappointment.

You choose to extend grace.[1]

---

1. Walker, Tim. "You Should Forgive Your Kids." *The Parent Cue*, September 1, 2014. Accessed March 26, 2026. https://theparentcue.org/you-should-forgive-your-kids/.

Here's what I am learning about forgiving others. Not only is it hard, but it is also humanly impossible, not for God, but for us.

It's a brain thing. Our brains are *not* designed to *choose to forgive*. There, I said it. Doesn't that make sense? Our brains are too beat up, and they trigger into fear cycles so quickly that we don't naturally forgive.

Only God forgives.

Only the Spirit of God in our inner being forgives. We need to stop trying to do it on our own and, instead, ask God to *make* us want to forgive. To *make* us be in sync with Him.

We can tell ourselves that forgiveness is a choice, and shame or berate people—or ourselves—into doing it better and more often, with very little fruit. GEPs know that forgiving others is a miracle of God, on par with the parting of the Red Sea, feeding the 5,000, or bringing something dead—like relationships—back to life.

It is one of the central tenets of the gospel. In fact, nothing is more core to the Good News. We are counting on God to forgive. I am.

Here's the good news/bad news:

God does it; we don't. In fact, there is a single Hebrew word for *forgiving*. There are several metaphors, but one single word. And guess what? Only God does it.

We *should* do it, and we should be good at it. Jesus says so. But we don't, and we are not. We can fake it, but it often proves ineffective and becomes a source of ongoing shame and failure.

I have spoken to many well-meaning Christians—teens among them—who know they are a disappointment to Jesus in this area.

Not only were they hurt by the perpetrator and still feel powerless; now they feel like failures, disappointments and weak, because they can't forgive once, much less 70x7 times.

Barna found that a quarter of Christians polled struggle to forgive something or someone.[2]

As a pastor for over 30 years, I have found that the number could be much higher than that.

Forgiveness therapists speak about cognitive and emotional forgiveness, meaning that the victim should groan, strain, and choose to forgive, give up the right to justice and revenge, and choose to empathize.

Perhaps you've heard something along those lines. Virtually 100% of secular and Christian books on forgiving say something to that effect. If there weren't a God and we didn't have the Spirit dwelling in our inner being, that would be all that was available to us.

But there is a God who forgives, and His forgiving Spirit is in our inner being.

Choosing to forgive on our own power sounds good and reasonable—even Jesus-like—but like so many of the other things involved with parenting, what muscle group do we use to do these things?

Our brains are not designed to give up justice—just the opposite. Our brains are designed to protect us from being hurt again, and we want justice—often obsessing over it for weeks, months, years or decades.

One of the first full statements that toddlers declare is, "But that's not fair!" It is in our God-imaged DNA.

And consider this: God never simply chooses to forgive. He never chooses to give up the right to justice. Never. That's what the Cross is all about. God doesn't forgive a single crime, hurt or rebellion until the Cross. Among other things, the Cross was a trial for

---

2. Barna Group, "1 in 4 Practicing Christians Struggles to Forgive Someone," April 11, 2019, https://www.barna.com/research/forgiveness-christians/.

all my shortcomings. God's forgiveness is a function of an experience of real justice.

He created us in His image.

So why, then, do we think that we can be even more magnanimous than God? Crazy.

Jesus says to forgive 7x70 times, but who does that?

Here's what I've found. In Matthew 18, Jesus says we are to forgive regularly and often, but He doesn't say how. Well-meaning people have filled in those blanks. I think we've messed that up big time.

There is so much more to say.

That's why I created the *Forgiving Path* (www.forgivingpath.com). It is a spiritual, online, evidence-based, experiential, gospel-intensive journey to help unforgiving Christians (and that's all of us) process those unresolved hurts, wounds, betrayals, crimes, disobedience, and lies— you know what I am talking about, parents.

It has helped over 1,000 people—including parents and teenagers.

In the end, I have seen the following miraculous changes. Remember, I will never ask you to choose to forgive, give up anything, or feel empathy toward the person who hurt you. And yet, look at the results. People who've gone through the Forgiving Path have reported noticeable changes. Here are the average numbers of all participants since June 2020:

- % Change in my desire to avoid the person who hurt me. Down 21.0%
- % Change in my sense of benevolence toward the person who hurt me. Up 38.2%

- % Change in my desire for revenge. Down 20.1%
- % Change in my experience of justice for the crime. Up 77.8%

Crazy results after only 2-3 hours.

Until you can begin to access God's forgiveness for your teen, demonstrated through your heart and voice, you can't do adolescent attunement well—not really. To your teen, it will still feel much closer to Still Face. You can't help it.

You have something against your teen. Your mid-brain's subconscious has taken that file out of memory, and it is an open case. Your teen can see it in your eyes. GEPs deal with that repeatedly.

But hear me. If you can access God's forgiveness for your teen, can you imagine the respect that your teen will feel—or at least see—in your measuring gaze? This is not reconciliation—that takes two miracles: forgiving that comes from God and godly sorrow that comes from God.

But your teen will feel respected by you. Remember, you are playing a long game.

GEPs understand that if they experience God's forgiveness for their teen, they will also be able to attune better with their teen, which will cause them to lean more toward Quadrant #1.

Review

Surprise! You can't forgive.

Forgiving a teenager who keeps wounding you feels impossible. Good news: it is impossible for humans. Only God forgives. The Spirit in you forgives.

That's why "just choose to forgive" leaves most Christians drowning in shame, if not a little angry.

The *Forgiving Path* (www.forgivingpath.com), a 2½-hour, evidence-based, gospel-intensive, online experience, has helped over 1,000 parents and teens who have gone through it.

When God's forgiveness flows through you, your teen will feel respected.

Tip #15

Good Enough Parents Remember the Main Thing More Than Non-Good-Enough Parents

(Your teen needs to know you're crazy about them—exactly as they are.)

Here we are at tip #15. Hopefully, these tips have encouraged you, given you some hope, and offered some baby steps toward becoming a more good enough parent. I trust I have not shamed you, knowing that you can't do it on your own—not well, not in the way you or your family deserve—any more than I could.

We all need to depend more on God's power so we can begin to grasp, feel, and experience the height, width, length, and depth of the love of Jesus toward us and toward our teens through us.

It's not about trying harder.

It is about admitting need and running to God with open hands repeatedly—the *SUG*.

This is how you access the *Main Thing*.

Mic-drop moment. To do the *Main Thing* well, you will need to admit that you can't do the *Main Thing* well—and run to Jesus for

His power. Do this, and your child may become and remain a good friend well into adulthood—taking a long view of parenting.

Early Childhood

In the first years of life and early childhood, your key role as a GEP is to attune with your baby girl or boy. The child's job is to discover the world. Both are great responsibilities.

Lean into being a good enough secure *base* for your child by being supportive, available, and sensitive to your child's needs—as perceived by your child—as well as caring for their biological needs. How? Ask God to make you in sync with His heart, and then be good enough.

Attunement, attunement, attunement—at least 30% of your interactions—three out of ten.

Some studies show that the most secure children are those whose parents regularly express joy when they see their children playing and exploring. Dance over your child more. God dances over His children.

"The LORD your God is with you, he is mighty to save. He takes great delight in you, he quiets you with his love, he rejoices over you with singing." (Zeph 3:17)

This is His DNA, and His Spirit is in your inner being. Ask God to make you in sync with Him—until you feel *good enough* joy over your child—at least more than you've been able to feel lately.

Middle Childhood

In middle childhood (ages six to eight), a biological switch is turned on as your child's adrenal glands become more active. This leads to elevated hormone secretion, which improves their learning of social scripts.

What is that? A social script is a series of behaviors that are expected in a particular situation, like a recipe for a slice of life. Think movie script.

An example of scripting would be going to the grocery store.

You park, get a cart, walk down the aisles, get what you need, check out, take your groceries to the car, load them, return the cart, and drive away.

This is a typical, expected scenario encountered when you go to the store, and it is a behavioral script that has developed over time.

Your child didn't come pre-equipped with these scripts. They really start adding to their scripts in middle childhood. "Let me do it, Mommy/ Daddy."

During this stage, your child is learning how to do life— learning scripts. Encourage and support them.

Dance over their discoveries.

Let them fail and have their backs.

"I can't tell you how proud I am of you."

This script building coincides with increased time spent away from the family (school, sports, clubs, hobbies, friends). Parents, prioritize being there for your child as their need for other types of parental support (enoughness and connectedness in school, relationships, and identity) increases and takes a new trajectory.

They will be experiencing new types of distress from the classroom, playground, interactions with others, bullying, conversations with children who are different from them, and dealing with fluid expectations from adults. Then there's the huge pressure put on your child's identity from social media.

But hear this, at this stage, your child does not need you to take over and solve all their problems for them (lawnmower or helicopter parenting).

Instead, shift from a handler to a coach who is vulnerable, who provides a safe place to talk and share feelings and thoughts, helps them process the distress, asks the right questions, and helps them see the difference between thoughts and emotions.

You may be familiar with the Cognitive Behavioral Therapy think-feel-do triangle.

When the time is right, you can propose solutions, but as much as possible, encourage your child to process your suggestions and develop their own, more than when they were younger. You are helping them become an adult—baby steps.

Of course, I am speaking about mildly distressing issues. These are those golden opportunities to let your child gain a little confidence and autonomy. Your job is more about being in a support role and communicating repeatedly just how big a fan you are—even when you disagree.

Watch as a thoughtful pre-adult begins to emerge—one who is taking baby-steps to make wiser life choices with growing confidence. And always communicate that you have their back—just like God has ours.

God adores us as we are, not as we should be or could be. This is true whether we get it right or mess up. GEPs tap into that amazing grace.

How? Ask.

Of course, if the situation and distress are more serious, if the parent has become the leading cheerleader and fan, the child will most likely be more motivated to seek out parental advice. This is golden when it happens. It is partly a function of the safe space you've created and protected. Good job.

Your child is becoming a more active partner in the process as you are regularly learning to dance over them.

Parent, you are leading the process.

You are their biggest fan.

They love seeing you smile when they walk into the room.

Keep asking God for His love for your little one.

Adolescence

The next stage, adolescence, ages nine to nineteen (tough gig). You are absolutely going to need the height, width, length, and depth of the love of Jesus for yourself and your child. By adolescence, I hope your child has begun to acquire some cognitive skills (and scripts), meaning they are thinking on their own.

But alongside that, there should remain a vibrant, accepted, safe-haven with parents and caregivers where the child knows that, in that space, they will be slathered with age-appropriate running kisses—no matter what.

They are going to need a great deal of support because now they are mostly away from home and doing a lot of healthy and unhealthy experimenting. That is what adolescents do.

They make mistakes. Their brain is asking the two all-too-important human questions:

One, "Am I worthy of your love?"

And two, "Can I count on you?"

They are subconsciously asking these questions over and over. God says to them, "Of course, absolutely; my Son purchased that for you." GEP, what do you say? Does your child know it?

The most well-adjusted adolescents will use their parents as a resource once they feel that they lack sufficient problem-solving capacity to process distress.

So, parents, we have a very difficult balancing act between giving our child space, allowing more autonomy, and remaining supportive, available, and sensitive to our child's needs.

Hard to do when they challenge you to your face, or walk out during dinner in a huff, or steal something, or experiment with pornography or drugs, or you are called to the principal's office for a myriad of reasons.

I get it.

GEP, stay in the game. Remember, your main job is to stay

consistently attuned to your child's emotional needs—their struggle with enoughness and connectedness—daily and weekly.

This attunement can only be accomplished when the child is confident that you adore them.

When they see you, does your face break out in a wide smile, eyes filled with joy, pupils dilated, just because they are there?

Are you still telling them that you are a big fan and would buy stock in them?

That you will always have their back, no matter what?

That you adore them as they are—not as they should be?

Remember the letter to you from God?

Remember the quote, "Every child needs at least one adult who is irrationally crazy about him or her." GEP, that can be you. Or at least you are one of those voices.

This is exactly what we need from our heavenly Father, isn't it? We deeply long to hear him say over us, "Well done, good and faithful servant. This is my beloved son or daughter with whom I am well pleased."

Hear the *SUG* one more time.

Jesus-follower, Parent or Guardian, strictly because of what Jesus did for you 2000 years ago, God loves you. He loves you with all His heart, as much as the Father loves the Son and the Son loves the Father. He can't love you any more or any less than He does right now—whether you think you've been a good enough parent or not. He loves you as you are, not as you should be or could be. You can't add to this love or take away from it. Now I get it, it often feels like you've messed it up or need to do something so God would like you better. How do you experience it more now? Simple! Good news, there is something you can do and are invited to do. You can take daily baby steps to ask the Spirit inside of you to make you know, experience, and feel just how much God loves you right now. Just ask. Ask again later today. Ask tomorrow. Make it a spiritual habit.

The *Main Thing* for GEPs? After fifteen tips, they all point to this. At every step along the way, make sure your child knows how much you adore them as they are, not as they should be or could be—not because they do this or don't do that—but because of who they are—your child. Not just words, but facial expressions, hugs and kisses. Being a child is difficult. Though parts of the brain are not fully online, their critical inner voice is active.

Don't miss this. There are three powerful competing voices in your cherub's brain: that critical inner voice, the voice of the Holy Spirit, if they are a Jesus follower, and then there is yours.

You don't have to be perfect. Lean into 30% of your reactions, that's doable, but only—ONLY—if you ask. I do not promote "Fake it until you make it." Children are very insightful.

Extra Tip#1
Good Enough Parents Know How to Evangelize Their Child More Than Non-Good-Enough Parents

"Preach the Gospel at all times; use words when necessary." St. Francis of Assisi.

"Do not tell them how to do it. Show them how to do it and do not say a word." Maria Montessori

"Don't talk about your philosophy, embody it." Epicetus

"In the same way, let your light shine before others, that they may see your good deeds and glorify your Father in heaven." Matt. 5:16

If the Holy Spirit is manifesting some of the 18 Tips through you, it will be noticeable. That is your greatest witness.

One of the basic principles of a *Good Enough Parent* is that, on your own, you can't do this job well. Your brain, and your child's, have been beaten up and badly rewired; it lacks the capacity to love the unlovable. Biblically, that is the state of all humans born after the Fall. To one degree or another, we are reactionary, not rational; self-focused, and unable to love or be loved well.

But here's the good news. The Holy Spirit in you is the opposite. As mentioned earlier, He innately loves the unlovable, the unloved, the unlovely, the unlikely, and the unworthy.

Paul was right! His letter to the Galatians is true of every human being on this earth since the Fall:

The acts of the sinful nature are obvious: sexual immorality, impurity and debauchery; idolatry and witchcraft; hatred, discord, jealousy, fits of rage, selfish ambition, dissensions, factions and envy; drunkenness, orgies, and the like. I warn you, as I did before, that those who live like this will not inherit the kingdom of God. (Gal 5:19-21)

We don't often use this language anymore. Suffice it to say, Paul just described a normal, red-blooded parent and teen. In some ways, it is not all our fault.

But good news. By the pursuing grace and rescue of God, you now have the Spirit of Christ in your inner being.

"But the fruit of the Spirit is love, joy, peace, patience, kindness, goodness, faithfulness, gentleness and self-control." (Gal 5:22-23a)

Historically, this has often been misunderstood; these are the fruit of the Spirit, not the fruit of you or me. We cannot produce these by trying harder. Sure, we can do better for a time, but that is not what Paul is referring to here.

He is speaking of motivations, desires, emotions, and actions that are innate only to God. We see them manifested more through us and through our actions when we ask:

"Holy Spirit, make your fruit flow through me—quickly—before I do something stupid and destructive again."

So, if your child happens to miraculously notice that you are more patient with them, less critical, less angry, less judgmental, less belittling, more loving of them as they are; if your drip, drip, drip of attuning is beginning to seep into their midbrains, if you are a little quicker to say "I'm sorry," or "I forgive you;" a natural question may seep into your child's prefrontal cortex:

"What is going on with mom? With dad? They seem different. More accepting, more loving, more excited to see me."

That's when you say this echo of the *Simple Uncluttered Gospel* from Tip #1.

Son/Daughter,

I need to tell you something. I'm really sorry. For a long time, I missed something important—and that affected you. I didn't fully understand what Jesus had already purchased for me, and because of that, I wasn't loving you the way I could have.

I'm beginning to understand that Jesus' love reaches the unlovable, the overlooked, the unlikely, and the unworthy—that's all of us, especially me. Through His Spirit, I'm starting to feel loved by God in a way I never have before. As that sinks in, I'm finding I can love others—including you—with more of His love.

I truly wish I had understood this sooner. Please forgive me. I hope it's not too late for us to grow into something better.

Here's what I'm learning: The Father, Son, and Spirit love me completely—fully—right now. Not because of what I do or don't do. Not because I get parenting right. It's not probationary. It's permanent. He can't love me more, and He can't love me less.

And because of that, I've been praying a new prayer. I ask the Spirit to make me feel that love deeply—and to make me love you from that place. Sometimes I pray, "Spirit, make me feel Your love right now. Make me rest in it. Make me live from it."

So, if you see me slipping back into old patterns, please let me know. Really. I want to keep growing.

I want you to know this: I appreciate you as you are. Not as you should be. Not as I imagine you could be. As you are. I believe in you. I'd buy stock in you.

We're going to disagree sometimes. That won't change. But this won't change either: I've got your back. Always.

Christian parent, you've got this.

Extra Tip #2
Good Enough Parents Encourage Their Children to Read Good Books More Than Non-Good-Enough Parents

"The Lord of the Rings is of course a fundamentally religious and Catholic work; unconsciously so at first, but consciously in the revision."
JRR Tolkien

Parents of teens and tweens often ask me why I write Christian fantasy books. Here's my answer: I write Christian young readers' quest books—a narrow sub-category within the larger fantasy genre—to change the world, one teen at a time.

I believe excellent Christian fantasy quest tales are beneficial for the developing brains of 10 to 16-year-olds and are an effective way to teach them about God's love for the unlovable.

Why Does This Matter Now?

I'm deeply concerned for the emotional and spiritual well-being of our tweens and teens.

What we're doing to evangelize and disciple them simply isn't working.

If you're a Christian parent or guardian of an adolescent, please don't dismiss this concern. Your child faces a bombardment of anxiety-inducing influences that no previous generation encountered. They need something more than weekly youth group Bible classes.

Remember, Jesus told stories—Kingdom-oriented stories. Your teen's brain is being flooded with competing stories, some of which are destructive to their well-being.

The crisis in numbers, acc ording to the CDC[1]:

- 42% of adolescents are experiencing sadness and hopelessness (up 50% from 2011).
- 46% of adolescents ages 13 to 17 say social media makes them feel worse about their body image.

We're facing a mental health crisis among our most vulnerable demographic. The time to shift our strategy for evangelizing and discipling adolescents is at a high point, now more than ever.

The Tolkien-Lewis Legacy

Reportedly, C.S. Lewis once said that if he had to do it all over again, he would write more young reader quest fantasy books like *The Chronicles of Narnia*. He understood their power for children and adults alike.

His dear friend, J.R.R. Tolkien—whom most credit as the father of the modern fantasy genre—believed God created our brains to thrive and expand when immersed in what he called "good fairy tales." This is what I've tried to embody in my *Kingdom Quest* series.

---

1. Centers for Disease Control and Prevention, "2021 Youth Risk Behavior Survey Results," last modified 2023, accessed May 6, 2026, https://www.cdc.gov/yrbs/results/2021-yrbs-results.html

The Two Diminished Camps

Unfortunately, most fantasy books written since Tolkien's *Lord of the Rings* trilogy fall into one of two problematic secular camps:

Camp 1: Formulaic "Hero's Journey"

In Camp 1, we see a stilted, highly formulaic storyline consisting of "a male central figure who triumphs over the forces of evil by innate virtue and with the help of a tutor or tutelary spirit."[2] These books claim to reflect Tolkien's philosophy but have greatly misunderstood his Christian Kingdom worldview.

Camp 2: Anti-Tolkien Nihilism

In Camp 2, we notice that the protagonists are wildly flawed and lead non-virtuous lifestyles. These books are often highly sexualized and rarely reconcile good and evil. They're not only unsuitable for 10 to 16-year-olds but can also be destructive.

What Makes Fantasy Truly Great

Brandon Sanderson, one of today's best-known fantasy writers, says good fantasy must include three things done well: world-building, story plotting, and character development. While Tolkien and Lewis would agree, they would also add reflecting the nature of God and the gospel as a very high priority.

This is what gives Tolkien-esque fantasies their unique spiritual framework and historic power to change young lives.

----

2. Jess of the Shire. *This Is Why We Never Got Another Lord of the Rings*. YouTube video, 9 Feb. 2024. Uploaded by Jess of the Shire. Accessed March 26, 2026. https://www.youtube.com/watch?v=_BBrDhgGz1k.

Historical Healing Through Story

Both Lewis and Tolkien wrote their quest stories partly to bring hope and emotional healing to the shattered teens of post-WWII Britain.

In the US, *The Lord of the Rings* trilogy exploded in popularity during the turbulent 1960s—an era of chaos, social unrest, new sexuality, Vietnam War fears, and horrific assassinations. The trilogy offered teens hope, the possibility of reconciliation between good and evil, and escape from surrounding chaos. This power of good fantasy to instill hope and healing is something we can harness for our teens today.

Even though the trilogy never explicitly mentions God, Jesus, the Holy Spirit, the Cross, or the gospel, these stories evangelized—or pre-evangelized—an entire generation.

The Science of Story

Research shows that being immersed in a good, positive story accomplishes something remarkably similar in a young teen to what occurs when a distressed infant is lovingly held in their mother's arms.[3]

Neuroscientist Gregory Berns explains:

Stories shape our lives and, in some cases, help define a person. The neural changes we found associated with phys-

---

3. Gregory S. Berns, Kristina Blaine, Michael J. Prietula, and Brandon E. Pye, "Short- and Long-Term Effects of a Novel on Connectivity in the Brain," *Brain Connectivity* 3, no. 6 (2013): 590–600; David Comer Kidd and Emanuele Castano, "Reading Literary Fiction Improves Theory of Mind," *Science* 342, no. 6156 (2013): 377–380; Raymond A. Mar, Keith Oatley, Jacob Hirsh, Jennifer dela Paz, and Jordan B. Peterson, "Bookworms versus Nerds: Exposure to Fiction versus Non-Fiction, Divergent Associations with Social Ability, and the Simulation of Fictional Social Worlds," *Journal of Research in Personality* 40, no. 5 (2006): 694–712.

ical sensation and movement systems suggest that reading a novel can transport you into the body of the protagonist. We already knew good stories can put you in someone else's shoes figuratively. Now we're seeing that something may also be happening biologically.[4]

The Neurological Benefits

Being immersed in a good story:

- rewires our brain and creates new positive neural networks.
- enhances communication between brain hemispheres.
- equips readers to process information more efficiently.
- can reduce stress levels by up to 68%.[5]

In as little as six minutes of reading, your heart rate slows, blood pressure lowers, and muscles begin to relax. Thirty minutes of daily reading dramatically impacts the physical symptoms of stress.

This is critical for the emotional, relational, identity, and spiritual well-being of our tweens' and teens' vulnerable brains, particularly during early adolescence (ages 9 to 19).

The Gospel Connection

When you add the gospel of Jesus's love to great storytelling—as Lewis and Tolkien discovered—something very significant happens. The protagonist and their quest should reflect Jesus' heart.

---

4. Gregory S. Berns, quoted in "Novel Finding: Reading Literary Fiction Improves Brain Connectivity," *Emory University News Center*, January 3, 2014.
5. David Lewis, *Galaxy Stress Research* (University of Sussex, 2009); B. Keles et al., "Social Media and Adolescent Mental Health," *International Journal of Adolescence and Youth* (2020).

The ending should manifest the God who works all things together for good.

Jesus, after all, is the Word, the story, that alone can rescue shattered, insecure, anxious, unlovable people in this broken world.

The Reading Crisis

Unfortunately, *reading for fun* levels have dropped:

- over 20% for 9-year-olds since the mid-80s.
- over 50% for 13-year-olds since the mid-80s.[6]

Reading has largely been displaced by screens, with social media being the most serious culprit. Unlike the positive benefits of reading good books, extended social media exposure is linked to higher anxiety, self-esteem issues, depression, eating disorders, and even suicide ideation.[7]

Not All Fantasy Is Created Equal

As Tolkien understood, not all fantasy books are the same. While some offer positive benefits, others might increase reader anxiety.

6. Jill Sonke et al., "Reading for Pleasure in the United States, 2003–2023," *iScience* (University of Florida and University College London study, 2025); National Literacy Trust, *Children and Young People's Reading in 2025* (London: National Literacy Trust, 2025).
7. Lauren E. Sherman et al., "The Power of the Like in Adolescence," *Psychological Science* 27, no. 7 (2016): 1027–1035; Eva H. Telzer et al., "Social Media Use and Neural Sensitivity to Social Rewards," *JAMA Pediatrics* 177, no. 3 (2023); Bekalu Keles et al., "Social Media and Adolescent Mental Health," *International Journal of Adolescence and Youth* 25, no. 1 (2020): 79–93; The Anxious Generation, *The Anxious Generation: How the Great Rewiring of Childhood Is Causing an Epidemic of Mental Illness* (New York: Penguin Press, 2024).

The story must include:

- a clear distinction between good and evil.
- a morally grounded protagonist.
- good conquering evil in the end.

Without these elements, adolescent readers won't experience the powerful emotional benefits and, instead, may experience increased anxiety and insecurity.

Tolkien's "Fairy Tales"

Tolkien's quest tales integrate the gospel framework into story-plotting, character development, and world-building. Such stories are the most powerful life-enhancing form of storytelling because of their ability to:

- Reawaken wonder at ordinary things around us.
- Empower anxious readers to escape from ugliness and foreboding.

Tolkien writes:

It is the mark of a good fairy story... that however wild its events, however fantastic or terrible the adventures, it can give to child or man that hears it, when the "turn" comes, a catch of the breath, a beat and lifting of the heart, near to (or indeed accompanied by) tears, as keen as that given by any form of literary art.[8]

---

8. J. R. R. Tolkien, "On Fairy-Stories," in *Tree and Leaf* (London: George Allen & Unwin, 1964), **67**.

A Glimpse of Gospel-Infused Fantasy

Here's an excerpt from the first book in my Kingdom Quest series, *Tale of the Unlikely Prince*. Notice the gospel shadows woven throughout.

Young, insecure Prince Yeled is sent on a great quest to validate his worth to the King. Unfortunately, his quest is an abysmal failure. His hopes of proving his worth to the Great King are dashed, and now he must face the King's disappointment. The Royal Vizier, Nomos, finds him on the road back to the castle to confess his failure to the King. Yeled—and the reader—must learn that not all quests are alike, and this King is definitely not what he appears.

Nomos: "Tell me, lad, how's the quest? Did you slay that nasty dragon?"

Yeled: "Nomos, with all due respect, I have failed badly. I have brought disgrace to myself and shame to my King. I am not worthy to be called his son."

Nomos paused, compassionately gazing into the young lad's eyes.

Nomos: "Oh, you foolish lad. You're not making any sense! I didn't ask about *those* dragons. I could care less about those insignificant reptiles. I asked if you slayed *the* dragon. That was your quest."

The Royal Steward invited the confused Yeled to sit on a nearby log.

Royal Steward: "My prince, inside your head lives a hungry dragon voraciously consuming almost every compliment, every statement of love, every honor. The beast quickly extinguishes any feelings of you being enough. Your dragon prevents you from feeling like the son any father would be proud of. Your quest was ultimately designed for you to face *that* dragon—*your* dragon."

Yeled: "How can I slay a dragon I can't see? How can I slay a dragon that *is* me?"

Nomos: "You can't. That's the whole point—the irony of it all. You can't. Now you have two paths: keep feeding your inner dragon for the rest of your life, never feeling good enough, or finally admit you can't do it and run helplessly to the arms of the King. There's real healing power there and there alone."

"The King knew you would fail, humanly speaking.

It was the goal of the quest. Sometimes such shaming is redemptive. Even failure in the careful hands of a wise King can lead to an end far greater than all successes combined. All you ever needed was need, and you didn't have that until now."

Do you hear the gospel? Your child will too. And they'll be able to share it with others.

The Ultimate Hope

Tolkien writes:

The consolation of fairy-stories, the joy of the happy ending... this joy is not essentially "escapist." It is a sudden and miraculous grace: never to be counted on to recur. It does not deny the existence of sorrow and failure... it denies universal final defeat and in so far is evangelium, giving a fleeting glimpse of Joy beyond the walls of the world.[9]

My ultimate hope is that our teens will reshape how they under-

---

9. J. R. R. Tolkien, "On Fairy-Stories," in *Tree and Leaf* (London: George Allen & Unwin, 1964), **68–69**.

 Dr. Bill Senyard

stand the gospel of the love of God for the unlovable, which, in turn, will affect how they share that gospel with their friends.

"Have you heard there's a God who cares for overlooked people like Gandalf did for the Hobbits? Or who has empathy for traumatized teens like the Lion in *The Lion, the Witch and the Wardrobe*—and even when they mess up, still ordains them Kings and Queens?"

Our teens are growing up in a world louder, faster, and more anxious than any generation before them. Stories are forming them—whether we intend it or not. My prayer is that we would be intentional about the stories shaping their hearts.

When story, beauty, and the gospel of grace come together, something powerful can happen.

A teen who feels insecure may begin to glimpse hope.

A child who feels unworthy may begin to imagine a different ending.

A discouraged heart may begin to believe that failure is not final.

That's why I care so deeply about this.

If this vision resonates with you—if you're looking for ways to disciple your teen not only through instruction but through imagination—I'd be honored to share more with you. I've written further about why Christian fantasy can be such a formative tool, and I'd gladly send you a free PDF called *Why Christian Fantasy?* Just email me at Bill@gospel-app.com.

And if you're exploring stories that reflect this kind of gospel-shaped framework, you can learn more about my *Kingdom Quest* series at www.drbillsenyard.com. The books were written with teens like yours in mind. We cannot control every voice speaking into our children's lives. But we can help choose the stories that shape their imaginations. And that is no small thing.

Extra Tip #3
Good Enough Parents Use the Shoulder Move More Than Non-Good-Enough Parents

I am going to have a little fun with a tactic I discovered from a Christian therapist. Parents, this tip will blow your mind.

I was speaking at a national Christian conference when one of the other speakers, Craig Miller, pulled me aside and indicated he had a helpful tip for parents. Craig is a seasoned author, speaker, Christian therapist, and social worker, and he has a great deal to say regarding healing prayer.[1]

Since then, I have adapted his *Love Hug* for Christian parents. I renamed it the *Shoulder Move* and hope it will help you attune to your adolescent more effectively.

Here is a description of how Craig uses it with adult clients. He begins with an audible prayer. Something like:

I pray that the eyes of my heart—our hearts—will be enlightened so that we will know what the hope of His

---

1. Craig A. Miller, *Breaking Emotional Barriers to Healing: Understanding the Mind-Body Connection to Your Illness*, foreword by Randy Clark (Winona Lake, IN: Whitaker House, 2018).

calling is, and what are the riches of the glories of His inheritance on us as His beloved children, and what is the surpassing greatness of His power toward us who have His Spirit dwelling in us.

I would suggest using our *Simple Uncluttered Gospel* (see Tip #1).

To facilitate openness and healing, Craig suggests that the hurting person enter a posture he calls the *love tap.*

He believes that the *love tap* triggers a brain response similar to that during REM sleep.

When we enter REM (rapid eye movement), our eyes dart back and forth repeatedly. Many believe it is the brain's way of reintegrating the right and left hemispheres while releasing the unhealthy anxieties, fears, injustices, and negative emotions of the day.

It is partly a form of emotional self-regulation.

Craig invites the person to cross their arms over their chest, rest their hands on their biceps, and imagine Jesus there, hugging them, with them, understanding them, adoring them as they are.

Then he invites them to gently pat their biceps, one hand at a time—right, left, right, left—in a slow rhythm, a little faster than a resting heartbeat.

With permission, he may gently place his right hand on their left shoulder and tap. As they continue to do love taps, he says to them:

This love tap naturally promotes the same biological functions created by God to help your mind sort through and release unwanted or blocked emotions and memories. It will encourage a sense of release, calm, and healing in your mind and body.

GEPs, I certainly wouldn't start at this level without first assessing your relationship with your child. Consider your child's comfort and trust level and adapt the shoulder move accordingly.

Remember, your teen can recognize a fake a mile away.

There may be a breakdown in trust, your child may have had a bad day, or your relationship with them may be tentative or shredded.

They may not feel safe with you. Building trust is essential before trying the shoulder move.

They may feel unlovable or unable to depend on anyone.

They lack enoughness and connectedness.

Their critical inner voice may be telling them that they are losers, broken, outies, unredeemable, odd ducks, or disappointments.

They may come to you with fear and trepidation, and they don't want you touching them or praying over them.

I wanted you to get an idea of the potential healing power, but trust and safety are key to your success.

So let's start with baby-steps for now and simplify the *Love Hug* for our purposes.

The Shoulder Move

Enter the *Good Enough Parent Shoulder Move*. With permission, gently put your right hand on your child's left shoulder, look them in the eyes, and offer a look of love, compassion, and grace—not criticism, judgment, or shaming—you know the difference.

They sure do.

This is level one of the baby-step shoulder move. Take the time to connect with your child. The point is to start somewhere. Look them in the eyes and tell them you will never leave them ("Can I count on you?"). And that you can't wait to see what will happen in their lives ("Am I lovable enough?").

Then say, "Good talk," and walk away.

You may have to leave a voicemail on their phone, text, or email them. You may be surprised how important that might be to your child in that moment.

"Daughter, son, I think you are going to change the world. I would buy stock in you. I can't wait to see who falls in love with you. They will be so lucky to have you."

In your context, decide what you want to say.

If your child is receptive, this might be a good time to ask them how they are doing.

What's up?

Just listen with genuine interest.

Really listen—no judgment.

Your child's reaction may be more emotional than rational, and that's okay. It's not all their fault. If they are avoidant like me, they may grunt, "Fine, can I go?"

Next-level shoulder move.

Start gently patting their shoulder. Craig has found that this stimulates sensory nerves that heighten your child's capacity to listen. It can make them feel comfortable and assured, and even begin to feel loved and somewhat lovable. It can also open them up to God's love —that's the big deal.

Then, looking them in the eyes, speak your heart over them:

Son, daughter, I understand you feel beat up right now. You feel like no one is there for you. You feel like a disappointment, and maybe you think that I am going to pile on. I am not. I want you to know that you will never be a disappointment to me. I will always be your greatest fan. There is nothing you can do to change that. You and I may—okay, *will*—disagree sometimes. You may even be right. But I will always be there for you. I believe you can change the world. I can't wait to see what God is going to do through you.

Then, if they are open, speak God's heart over them:

I know you know this, but I must be reminded of it every day, particularly when I feel beat up, overlooked, and unlovable. Because of what Jesus did for you and me 2,000 years ago, God adores us, as we are. He is not disappointed in us. We haven't messed it up. He is here right now, hugging us. He is so proud of you. I am too.

I wanted to remind you of that. Now, what can I do for you?

I hope this helps. Give it a shot.

I love hearing your stories about the *shoulder move*. (Bill@gospel-app.com)

~

In Closing

Good Enough Parent, if you remember nothing else from this book, remember this: your child does not need a perfect parent. They need a parent who is willing to depend on a perfect God.

The adolescent years are loud, emotional, confusing, and often exhausting—for them and for you.

There will be slammed doors, hard conversations, failures, regrets, tears, awkward prayers, and moments when you feel utterly inadequate.

But none of those moments have the power to separate you or your child from the love of Christ.

Your job was never to save your child, perfectly regulate every emotion, or carry the weight of the entire story on your shoulders. Your calling is simpler—and harder.

Stay present.

Stay dependent upon the Holy Spirit in your inner-being.

Keep looking up into the smiling face of God so that your child has a better chance of seeing His delight reflected in yours. That alone will shape more than you realize.

So breathe, weary parent.

Exhale the shame.

You were always going to get this wrong sometimes. That is why grace exists.

The Spirit is already at work in your Christian child's life in ways you cannot see, measure, or control. Even the groaning, the chaos, the uncertainty, and the waiting are part of a bigger redemption story still unfolding.

Good Enough Parents are not fearless, flawless, or endlessly patient. They are simply parents who keep returning to Jesus with emptier hands and greater dependence. And over time, that dependence becomes noticeable: a little softer gaze, a little less reactivity, a little more peace, a little more courage, a little more love. Not perfection. Just enough grace for today—and then enough grace again tomorrow.

If your cup is filled with the Holy Spirit in you, you will need to fill your cup less from your child, their response to you, and their behavior.

That is a huge deal.

Now What?

From all the tips in GEP, find the three or four that fit your context and run with them.

Don't feel like you need to do them all.

Decide on a few and do them intentionally.

In the meantime, keep saying the *SUG* aloud, twice a day, for your own spiritual self-care. You are preaching the gospel to that unreached people group in your midbrain that keeps telling you that you are a failure as a parent and that God is disappointed in you.

That is not true.

Take heart, child of God.

Discussion Questions

Tip #1: Good Enough Parents Experience the *Simple Uncluttered Gospel* More Than Non-Good-Enough Parents

1. When you hear "God permanently invites you to the dance, and He can't love you more or less," what feelings arise first—relief, skepticism, tears, something else? How can you practically remind yourself of this truth during challenging parenting moments and remain rooted in the gospel?
2. On a scale of 1–10, how often do you wake up feeling God's delight in you, rather than just knowing it?
3. Have you said the *SUG* prayer out loud twice a day for a week? What small shifts did you notice in your heart or attitude?
4. What lie does your inner critical voice scream the loudest when parenting gets difficult?

Tip #2: Good Enough Parents Access the Power of the Gospel More Than Non-Good-Enough Parents

1. Paul had to ask for power to feel Christ's love in a hostile culture. How is parenting teens today similar to living in first-century Ephesus?
2. When was the last time you felt completely emptied by your child? Did you ask God to *fill you* right then, or did you power through?
3. Have someone pray Ephesians 3:14-21 aloud over you. What did you notice in your body?

Tip #3: Good Enough Parents Understand Their Own Brain More Than Non-Good-Enough Parents

1. Spock or Kirk—who was driving when you lost it with your teen this week?
2. Under stress, what's your go-to fight/flight/freeze response—yell, withdraw, shut down, sarcasm?
3. How does knowing "there's no muscle group for this" free you from the trying-harder trap?

Tip #4: Good Enough Parents Understand Their Teen's Brain More Than Non-Good-Enough Parents

1. Which of the two big questions does your teen seem to ask most: "Am I enough?" or "Am I connected?"
2. When your teen is dysregulated, how easy is it to remember, "This is brain chemistry, not just rebellion?"
3. If you could go back and whisper one truth to your

teenage self regarding the two questions ("Am I enough?" and "Am I connected?"). What would it be?

Tip #5: Good Enough Parents Are Aware of the Power of Attunement More Than Non-Good-Enough Parents

1. Honest check-in: on a 0–10 scale, where would you rank your attunement during your child's first two years? (No shame—just curiosity.)
2. Which life circumstances made 30% attunement hard back then?
3. How does knowing adolescence is God's built-in "second chance" reshape how you view today's chaos?

Tip #6: Good Enough Parents Have an Attuning "Gaze" More Than Non-Good-Enough Parents

1. After watching the *Still Face* video, what emotions stood out most?
2. When your teen walks into the room, what does your face communicate first?
3. What's one small way you could let your eyes "light up" more this week?

Tip #7 & #8: Good Enough Parents Are More Aware of Their Teen's Attachment Style Than Non-Good-Enough Parents

1. Look at the four quadrants. Which quadrant best describes your teen? Which describes you?

2. Which insecure quadrant described you growing up?
    How does that show up in your parenting?
3. What's one behavior you could start—or stop—that
    would feel more *security-building* to your teen?

Tip #9: Good Enough Parents Teach and Model for Their Teens How to Preach the Gospel to Themselves

1. What's the last disruption in your home that remains
    unrepaired?
2. Which part of the repair is the hardest: owning your part,
    naming their feeling, or re-attuning?
3. Who's willing to attempt one repair this week and report
    back?

Tip #10: Good Enough Parents Are More Aware of Their Own Attachment Styles Than Non-Good-Enough Parents

1. When your teen is upset, are you more likely to fix,
    lecture, minimize or simply stay present?
2. What's the last time you listened until your teen felt fully
    heard? How did it go?
3. Think of a recent conflict with your teen. How was your
    attachment style manifested? How was theirs?

Tip #11: Good Enough Parents Understand Adolescent Attunement Better Than Non-Good-Enough Parents

1. What's one recent thing your teen did (even something
    tiny) that deserves over-the-top celebration?

2. When did you last tell your teen—out loud and specifically—that you're proud of who they are, not just what they do?
3. Challenge: Send one "I'm ridiculously proud of you because ____" text to your teen before the next meeting.

Tip #12: Good Enough Parents Know How to Deal with Teen Conflict More Than Non-Good-Enough Parents

1. When consequences are needed, which feels more natural: protecting the rule or protecting the relationship?
2. Share a time you chose relationship over being *right*. What happened long-term?
3. How does *firm boundaries* + *warm connection* feel different from permissive or authoritarian parenting?

Tip #13: Good Enough Parents Apologize More than Non-Good-Enough Parents

1. Do you default to "worldly sorry" or "godly sorry" with your teen?
2. Who needs to hear a godly-sorrow apology from you this week?
3. Pray the godly-sorrow prayer out loud together now for a specific hurt you may have caused.

Tip #14: Good Enough Parents Forgive More than Non-Good-Enough Parents

1. What's the one thing your teen has done (or keeps doing) that's hard to release?
2. Have you ever tried *choosing to forgive* in your own power and ended up more bitter? What happened?
3. Who's willing to go through the *Forgiving Path* this month and share what shifted?

Tip #15: Good Enough Parents Remember the Main Thing More Than Non-Good-Enough Parents

1. When your teen walks into the room tomorrow, what do you want your face to communicate before you say anything?
2. If your teen could only hear one sentence from you for the rest of their life, what would you want it to be?
3. Close by going around the circle: "(Teen's name), I'm so glad God gave you to me because _____."

Extra Tip #1: Good Enough Parents Know How to Evangelize Their Child More Than Non-Good-Enough Parents

1. How does recognizing that the fruit of the Spirit flows through you—not from you—change the way you approach moments of conflict, frustration, or disappointment with your child? Can you identify a recent moment when relying on the Spirit might have changed your response?

2. St. Francis, Maria Montessori, and Epictetus all
   emphasize showing rather than telling. How can you
   practically "preach the gospel" to your child through
   your daily actions and attunement, rather than words?
   What small, noticeable behaviors might communicate
   the gospel more effectively than a lecture?

3. The text models a parent acknowledging mistakes and
   sharing their journey of understanding God's love.
   How could honestly expressing your own growth,
   struggles, and reliance on God help your teen
   internalize a sense of enoughness and connectedness?
   Are there ways to do this without causing them guilt or
   shame?

Extra Tip #2: Good Enough Parents Encourage Their Children to Read Good Books More Than Non-Good-Enough Parents

1. How have the stories your child consumes—books,
   movies, or games—shaped their sense of self, morality,
   or understanding of the world? Are there examples
   where a story has given them hope, courage, or insight?

2. Considering the power of gospel-infused fantasy, how
   can you intentionally introduce your teen to books that
   model God's love, moral courage, and emotional
   healing? What steps can you take to make these stories a
   natural part of their reading habits?

3. In the *Unlikely Prince* quest story, Yeled learns about
   failure, self-worth, and the King's redeeming love. How
   could reading similar stories help your child internalize
   the gospel and develop a sense of enoughness and
   connectedness that isn't dependent on external approval?

Extra Tip #3: Good Enough Parents Use the Shoulder Move More Than Non-Good-Enough Parents

1. How could you adapt the baby-step version of the shoulder move in your daily interactions with your teen? What's one small way to show love and attunement without overwhelming either of you?
2. Why are trust and permission so important before using the shoulder move? How might your teen's past experiences influence their openness to physical or verbal expressions of love?
3. How can speaking God's love over your child—through words, gaze, or touch—reinforce their sense of enoughness and connectedness? Can you identify moments where this could be particularly healing or transformative for your teen?

If this has been helpful, get the word out to other parents. Imagine a whole community doing GEP. It would be noticeable.

Lastly, I genuinely value feedback—it helps this message grow. Reach me at **Bill@Gospel-App.com**.

For speaking engagements, workshops, or training inquiries, feel free to reach out.

Also In the Good Enough Series

Let's be honest. A lot of Christians are exhausted. You believe the gospel. You show up. You try to do the right things. And yet—your faith still feels thin. Distant. Underwhelming.

So you start to wonder…

"Is something wrong with me?"

Good Enough Christian offers a different answer: Maybe it's *not* all your fault.

In this honest and hope-filled book, Dr. Bill Senyard explores why so many sincere believers struggle to actually experience God's love—and what can finally change that. You'll learn:

• Why trying harder doesn't work

• How your brain quietly resists grace

• What's really blocking your experience of Jesus' love

• Why the Holy Spirit—not your effort—is the key

This isn't about becoming a better Christian. It's about discovering that, in Christ…You already are.

~

Let's be honest.

Most Christians feel like they're not very good at prayer. You've tried the methods, the acronyms, the quiet times.

And yet—your prayer life still feels forced, inconsistent, or nonexistent.

So you quietly assume:

"I must be doing something wrong."

Good Enough Prayer offers a different answer:

Maybe prayer was never meant to work that way.

In this refreshingly honest book, Dr. Bill Senyard walks through twenty of the Bible's most unfiltered prayers—showing that God isn't looking for polished words or perfect performance.

God is inviting something else entirely.

You'll learn:
- Why prayer often feels so hard (and why it's *not* all your fault)
- What the Bible's Top 20 prayers reveal about God's heart
- How to stop performing and start relating
- Why experiencing God's love is the key—not trying harder

This isn't about becoming a prayer warrior.

It's about becoming a child who knows they're already heard.